Foreword

From the *Readers*

At the end of "doing" that is that. If the self is backed into a corner (successfully calling into question its separateness), it will be in crisis. Then something has to happen. Maybe in some that will be surrender. I think reading this book may well back some selves into corners.

Reading this "book" is like a giant ball of multi-colored yarn. You begin to unravel it slowly and by the time you get to the end of the yarn there is just "you" hanging on to a small thread.

This book is a valiant attempt to explain the ineffable. The author's ability to draw from both modern and ancient sources to weave together a "workable" deconstruction of the Self is both timely and deeply insightful.

Having read this book I can only say it brought me to a realization about the workings of the Ego which I had never known. It has made my life less of a drama, or at least I am aware when I am creating the drama and I am able to observe it rather than fully engage in it.

Words always fail to express

what is inexpressible. Words

approach it and then fall

backwards. Additional words fail

again..

Words create ideas;

numerous words produce

numerous ideas.

You believe you were born into

this world. It is not so..

We each create a world for

ourselves. You inhabit it, and

find it unrewarding.

Your world is filled with wants,

aversions, fears and plans to

avoid fear.

Don't you see this is your private

world? It is just in your mind.

Once you see that this is insane;

you are beginning to be free of it.

Daoist Philosopher

300 BC

Introduction

I hate books that start off with a long introduction that usually includes an autobiography of how the author got from "there" to "here" wherever that "here" might be. The truth seems to be that it does not matter in the least where the author was "in the beginning".

There is no beginning, no ending, and no arriving! Somehow this description of the author's journey to Enlightenment, or Awareness, or whatever you want to call it, always seems to me to be more about the authors Ego than the Awareness.

So I generally find the introduction boring and self-serving, and go right to the main course of the book.

It doesn't matter at all what my childhood experiences may have been, nor does it matter what my journey was up until this point. It doesn't matter what I do for a living, or what my current life situation is. All that matters (to me at least) is what I call my *Undoing*.

I hope you have this *Undoing* experience as well, although it may seem quite scary. Many people talk about this experience beginning to occur after a major loss in life, a time where what they thought offered them some type of security suddenly was gone.

Sometimes this experience begins spontaneously without any observable precipitating factors. Sometimes it begins when someone is involved in some type of altered states experience like yoga, or meditation, or other contemplative spiritual practice.

Throughout the ancient writings of the various spiritual traditions this Undoing is identified in many ways. Advaita Vedanta, the Kabbalah, the Buddhist emptiness teachings, Gnostic Christianity, and modern non-dual teachers like Eckhart Tolle, Rupert Spira and others all point to this experience of undoing, this experience in which awareness arises and you know you are not your body-mind Ego state.

You are aware that who you thought you were is not who you are. You are aware that what you thought was "reality" isn't. You are aware you don't really have a past or a future. You are aware that there is simply what is happening now, right this minute. You are aware that labels for things are just that. Labels are just words that mean very little in terms of the true nature of things.

And you become aware that separateness is an illusion of this thing we call a "mind"

This Undoing is not something YOU do! It is something you become aware of. It is the awareness that there is simply one consciousness, one experience that is always happening, and you become aware that you are simply that experience, always unfolding. And mostly you become aware that there is really no way to explain this with words and concepts, although of course we try!

Stanislav Grof, psychiatrist and the father of the Transpersonal psychology movement describes this as one of the experiences that can precipitate a spiritual emergency.

In Western psychiatry and clinical psychology this experience might be "explained" with definitions of pathology like depersonalization, derealization, etc... (Of course those who are labeling the Undoing experience as pathological are generally individuals who have not had this Undoing experience).

In any event no matter what labels (spiritual, pathological, or whatever) are used in an attempt to define it, it can't really be defined because it is experience beyond the thinking, labeling, intellectual mind.

So read on, and put your mind (and your fear) aside for the time being. Don't worry, you can pick up your mind (and your fear) anytime you want to.

I have asked some colleagues to be *The Reader* of this book as it unfolds, and comment on their experience of the reading. Some of those comments will be included throughout the book identified as *The Reader*.

I do this not only because I respect their opinions, but also it may give you a sense of what someone else experiences along with you as you hopefully unfold along with the book.

Some of their comments will be as a question. I will not attempt to answer *The Readers* questions as the questions simply point to further inquiry as the reader deconstructs the Self.

Just so you know, this "book" has 25,000 words. That's a lot of words...so it does appear to be a book.

Chapter 1: What We Generally Believe.

Realize that all of your perceptions
are subjective. All that is
thought, felt, heard, smelled, or felt,
perceived or imagined, is
simply an illusion.

You may be a very unique and special person who does not experience "life" as I am about to describe, but I think I can safely say that most of us believe the following most of the time.

We believe we live in a world in which there is security, safety, and logical reasons for things. We also believe that our "mind". is somewhere in our bodies (usually the head) and that our mind is the source of our thinking and our emotions.

"I think therefore I am."

We believe that in this orderly mind-body, our thoughts create our feelings. If I think "positive" thoughts I will feel good, and if I think "negative" thoughts I will feel bad.

We also believe we are the *Doer* of the body's actions and that our actions are determined by us (the *Doer).*

We believe that our mind-body is separate from other mind-bodies; that we are all separate entities trying to achieve security and safety through various actions (getting a degree, finding a good job, buying a house, finding that right person who will be there for us and complete us, etc..).

Since we believe resources are limited we then see other separate entities as our competitors (for the good job, the right house, or that special person). Others become a threat to us achieving security.

When we feel threatened we attack either directly or indirectly. We perpetuate "attack thoughts" and we assume others are doing the same.

So here we are in this separate body, fighting for security. We also realize at a deeper level that we can (and eventually do) lose whatever security we have fought so valiantly for (the job ends, the house has to be sold or deteriorates. that special person leaves us or dies).

And we are terribly afraid of death because we perceive this event as losing all that we are and have accumulated.

Life has now become a constant state of anxiety, holding on to what security we think we have, trying to get more of it, defending against losing it, and still realizing that eventually we will lose it no matter what we do!

We may not be consciously aware that we are in this constant state. We can say we are "stressed" or "careful" or that we plan thoroughly, or whatever.. but the truth is.. if you look a little deeper... you're terrified. Terrified of life, terrified of death, just plain ole terrified.

So to try and reduce this *existential* anxiety we may obsessively hold on tight to what we have, develop elaborate schemes to deny our perceived reality, drink or do drugs, get more degrees, spend a fortune on plastic surgery, there are many ways to temporarily try and deceive ourselves.

We develop shared political, philosophical and religious delusions to convince us that we really are secure and protected from "the enemy".

We are constantly on alert, scanning our environment for any evidence of a threat. This has become our life.

We are very uncomfortable with uncertainty. Things need to have labels, put in their little boxes, or all hell will break loose. We feel we have to be able to determine what is good/bad, right/wrong, better/worse, friend/foe, up/down, far/near, comfortable/uncomfortable, healthy/unhealthy.

We live by labeling opposites. If we cannot label something we deny it, denigrate it, or destroy it. No grey area here..not for long anyway.

Just think about the labels *good/bad* and *right/wrong* for a moment. I challenge you to identify any form, object, or event (person, place or thing) and *not* label it at some level as either good/bad or right/wrong (you may use less specific terms, but it's still the same thing).

I think if you are truthful with yourself, you can't do it.

The Reader: This is exactly the problem of looking without thinking, observing without the observer. Right at the heart of the matter.

If you find this state of labeling to be true for you, take a moment to realize this is your *constant state of thought.* Exhausting, isn't it! And what are you basing these determinations on?

Time is simply defined to be what our clocks measure. They define the time standards for the globe. Time is defined by the number of clicks of their clocks.

Einstein, for one, found solace in this revolutionary sense of quantum time. In March 1955, when his lifelong friend Michele Besso died, he wrote a letter consoling Besso's family; "Now he has departed from this strange world a little ahead of me. That means nothing. People like us, who believe in physics, know that the distinction between past, present and future is only a stubbornly persistent illusion."

Hhmmm...a "stubbornly persistent illusion" Einstein says... so maybe, just maybe we who are on the "right side" (Of course there is a past, present, and future) are in actuality, on the "wrong side".

See, these "right side" and "wrong side" concepts are pretty useless.

The Reader: This is why we can't see what is in the present, because we are always in the past or the future.

And now, back to seeing things as they really are.

Try this experiment out. Look at anything you see in the present. Are you actually "seeing" whatever you are looking at in the present? For example, let's say you are looking at a ceramic jug. How do you know that jug would hold water?

You would have to be thinking back to a past experience with that, or another similar ceramic jug. You would have to have, at some point in the past, poured water into that jug or a similar one, and the water didn't leak out.

You have an image in your mind of that past experience. Your perception of that jug is simply a thought about a past experience.

I would suggest that all of your current perceptions are simply thoughts about the past. Try this one out for awhile. You may need to play with it to see that it is true.

The Reader: I think knowledge like how jugs work is different than the opinions about our self in time.

We can call the things we see within our visual field "forms". I would like to suggest that every form you see is actually past thoughts. Don't freak out, or put the book down... just stay with it.

While we are on this topic of perception, we also believe that thoughts and images are separate things. I would like to suggest that all thoughts are actually images of the past that you have created. Try it out. Think any thought you like. Can you have that thought without images from the past arising in your "mind"? I don't think so.

Remember above that your "present" perception is based on thoughts about past experiences. Thoughts/ images, images/thoughts. You can't have a thought without an image arising, and images are based on past experiences. If this is confusing you, you're on the right track. It get's worse before it gets better!

What else do we believe.. let's *see..* we have millions of beliefs. Let's just cover the first few thousand. Beliefs, opinions, attitudes...they're all just thoughts made up by you.

One of our primary and most forceful beliefs is that we are somehow different, unique or special. Some of us were told that growing up, weren't we? We're not. Although your "form" that you see in your visual field may appear differently than my "form" externally, there is no difference (remember what you see and the images you create are simply perceptions of the past).

David Bohm, an amazing physicist of our time said this in his book *Wholeness and the Implicate Order:*

"It will be ultimately misleading, and indeed wrong, to suppose…that each human being is an independent actuality who interacts with other human beings and with nature. Rather, all these are projections of a single totality."

And one again, our friend Einstein said, in reference to this topic of separateness:

"A human being is part of the whole that we call the universe, a part limited in time and space. He experiences himself, his thoughts and feelings, as something separated from the rest- a kind of *optical illusion of his consciousness*. This illusion is a prison for us, restricting us to our personal desires and to affection for only the few people nearest us. Our task must be to free ourselves from this prison by widening our circle of compassion to embrace all living things and all of nature."

The only way to try and be "different" from the form next to you is by using your thoughts to create separation and to label with words (taller/shorter, male/female, fatter/thinner, etc...).

These are just words which that large group of people has decided is objective truth.

The words do not actually mean anything but are used by one form as a mental tool to create separation from another form. And we do all want to be separate and unique, don't we? (Do we really??)

In actuality, your form and that form called a "table" are no different, but that's for a later section of the book.

In order for this experience to be a "book" I believe it is supposed to have a beginning, middle, and an end. So I would think I need to "end" this chapter and "begin" another one or it wouldn't be this thing we call a book, so I'll do that now.

Of course, by now, you may be asking, "When is he going to present the *Undoing*?

Maybe in the next chapter he will get to the point! Those who are astute will notice already that this isn't a typical book. There really isn't a beginning, middle and an end. Who said it was supposed to be a logical progression? Certainly not I!

Are you back into that old past, present and future thing again? By the way, I have already been sneaking in aspects of the *Undoing*.

Chapter II: The Next Chapter

KNOWING and the Ego

It is only when the intellect is
completely confused that a clear
mind can exist.

Apparently there is supposed to be a next chapter since, in this logical progression, there is now a chapter before this. So this must be the next chapter.

Probably at this point you are either bored, terribly confused, wishing you hadn't paid for this book, or you are "getting it". It is impossible to define what "getting it" actually is.

All I can say is that if you're "getting it" you know it. If you're not "getting it", either you will or you won't as you keep reading. Who knows!

Notice your emotional reaction as you read the paragraph above. What did you feel? If you're starting to "get it" you may feel some initial excitement, some "aha" experience even if fleeting.

If you're not "getting it", you are probably feeling either duped or irritated. Either way, you more than likely are expecting something really profound to be revealed sooner or later.

So what we can look at here is the need to KNOW.

We need to KNOW something. And we expect that if we don't know it, there is something to DO to get to that knowing. Most of us in the KNOWING mode believe that gaining more information, having a greater intellectual understanding, studying, analyzing, THINKING, will produce the KNOWING.

The Reader: Is knowing something possible? Why would we question the ability to know something? It seems like the idea of knowing and the idea that all forms are the same thing, differentness is not possible, are mutually exclusive.

Based on the last chapter, we can probably deduce that thinking will not get us there. An intellectual understanding and analyzing will not get us there. (Where is it we are supposed to be going, anyway?)

This all points to the way the Ego mind/separate self works. It's based on seeking but not finding.

If it finds, it won't be necessary any more! It's based on not being OK! It's not comfortable with just being. It has to strive, to do, to become something better and greater, achieving, getting somewhere.

The Ego mind hates concepts like "Just be", "Don't strive", "Let things unfold as they do","Open to the present moment", etc.

The Ego mind can never be in the present moment. It always wants to get to somewhere better. It's never OK with what is. There has to be a purpose, a goal, a future, something just around the corner that will make it worth it.

The Ego mind's major goal is *not OKness.* Somehow, KNOWING more, in the future, will make it Ok. It always implies that what you know now isn't enough. There has to be more, bigger, better, soon!

The Reader: I actually think Okness is what the ego is generally trying to get – that is security. But how can there be security with all the competing, separate demands for security. Isn't separateness the tool? Maybe this is a chicken and the egg question.

Does this sound like anyone we know? Check out the mirror.

Remember the Ego mind is built on separateness. That is its goal, function, and purpose.

The Reader I wonder if separateness is the goal. It seems separateness is the product of time and the deep desire for security for itself.

This separateness can only be sustained by the Ego mind by being judgmental (creating judgments of yourself and others). In order to be separate there has to be comparison. "I'm smarter/dumber, cuter/uglier, faster/slower, thinner/fatter, than _____."

The Reader: Comparison, measuring is how the self determines where it is at, how safe it is.

Without comparison there would not be separateness, and the Ego mind has no intention of letting go of separateness, otherwise it would not exist.

The Ego mind doesn't really care whether you're judging you and others in a positive or negative light, as long as you're seeing yourself as different (separate) from other forms.

It's focused on process, not content.

The Reader: It seems the self cares a lot about whether it is judging itself or others as good or bad. Selves get sick and dies around these judgments.

The Reader: I think we can't avoid that change doesn't happen to "me". Deepening awareness that we (several I's) are not who we thought, but who we really are." I think this is the problem of duality and not just semantics. I cannot become "that" perhaps "that" can clear up me.

I remember a woman in one of the groups I facilitate, having heard the above statement, say "Ok, now I "get it". I understand how the Ego operates, so what do I DO now to change it?" (She didn't "get it.").

It's not about doing, changing, or fixing IT.

What it's actually about is being aware of, observing, this Ego state. It's not really a thing, a separate entity. It's simply a way of misperceiving reality. A habitual misperception that we are very attached to and very comfortable with although it makes us very uncomfortable.

The Reader: Who or what is aware, what observes "this ego state"? This is a foreign concept to me... that something besides me can be aware in the space or consciousness that the me usually occupies

What we begin to become aware of by simply observing this state is that it begins to lose it's foothold on our misperceived reality. We simply begin to see our experience differently.

The Reader: Can "I" be aware of something separate from thought? Can thought be aware? Am I (the ego) separate from thoughts made out of memories? If it is something different than memories then what is that separate I?

Notice that we cannot be the Observer and the observed at the same time. By observing we may actually begin to see our true reality for the first time!

The Reader: I'm wondering can I/we be anything but the observer and the observed at the same time. What is "our true reality", the group's, humans? The I observes and feels it is watching something else, that there are two things, the observer and the observed. This observing something else is how there gets to be separateness.

But a note of warning! This can be a very uncomfortable, destabilizing experience at first. In a sense we also begin to grieve what we thought was reality, our sense of self as the *Doer* who is "in charge" of things.

We begin to see this Ego state as rather useless in the big picture.

But that is for another chapter...

Chapter III: Another Chapter.

What We Can Choose to Perceive.

The fear of not being anything in
particular stops us from
seeing things clearly.
When you come into direct contact
with nothingness you
realize it cannot do you damage.
You see the illusion of
fear and allow it to vanish.

As stated earlier (I think) some people, but very few I believe, have this experience of perceiving things differently as one gigantic life changing event. I don't think that is how most of us regular people experience it. For most of us it's one tentative change in perception at a time.

The Reader: Why is this? Why doesn't it just end? What keeps it going, even after a moment of "selflessness"?

One step forward, three steps back as they say (although in Reality, there are no steps). For many of us this Ego/separate/"I'm in charge" state of misperception holds on like an Anaconda wrapped around us.

Each time we take a breath toward freedom, it tightens its grip. Yes, sooner or later it's either the true me or the Anaconda in a life or death battle, but it may be possible to slowly loosen its grip so we can begin to untangle ourselves a bit.

The only choice we really can make is how we choose to perceive reality on a *minute by minute* basis. Yep, that's it... the only choice we really can make and have to make. And yes, it is true; this minute really is the only time we have.

Remember that past, present, and future we talked about earlier? Interesting *concepts* of time don't you think? Let's take a look at that. Remember concepts are just groups of thoughts around a central theme, similar to theories about how things "really are".

We can agree that theories are just possible explanations for how things are but we tend to believe for some reason that concepts are true!

Let's look at a dictionary definition of concept:

1. a general notion or idea.

2. an idea of something formed by mentally combining all its characteristics or particulars; a *construct*.

3. a directly conceived or intuited object of thought.

Hhmm...notions, ideas, mentally combining, object of thought. What are you seeing here?

A concept is simply more thoughts, and thoughts are derived from the Ego state. Kind of a circular process wouldn't you say? So now let's look more closely at this concept of time.

Time is a mental *construct*. There is no "objective" reality to it. As a matter of fact it is very subjective. Have you ever been to a really boring movie, lecture or other event and it seemed like it was lasting forever?

Time seems to be standing still, no matter how much you wish this thing would end, it just seems to be lasting forever.

Now let's assume you took a friend to that same event and he or she is sitting next to you. He or she for some reason you cannot fathom really loves this kind of event.

To your relief, as the event finally comes to and end, he or she may say to you, "It seems like it went by so fast! I could have stayed here for another six hours!" Now, whose perception of "time" is accurate? (Yours, of course!).

The point being, psychological time is totally up to the perceiver. Yes, most of us have these things on our wrists called watches which tick off a certain number of minutes and hours. But a day, with hours and minutes in it, is just a made up concept shared by a majority of people based on the effects of the Sun.

When we think of it this way, we can see there is no objective truth to time, we made it up!

The Reader: Can the self exist without time? Without the past? Without the past how would the self prepare for a secure, comfortable future, with all the things the self 'needs' to be OK.

With this in mind, let's look at two other concepts we made up within this made up concept of time; *past* and *future*. Get ready for this one....there is really no such thing as past and future except in our minds. And our minds are only in operation NOW.

Really think about this for awhile. (I'll *time* you for 5 minutes). We are ONLY having thoughts NOW! They may be thoughts that we label as past, or future, but we are only thinking NOW. It's always NOW.

We may be having a thought NOW that says, "I had a crappy childhood" or "next week I will be on vacation", but the truth is, it's only NOW.

Thoughts that we label as "about the past" or "about the future" are just thoughts we are having in the present moment. So we may have the thought, "I had a crappy childhood" and then follow that thought with another one that says, "And that's why I'm so dysfunctional now!", and follow that thought with, "And that's why I'll never be happy in the future", but those are all just thoughts you are having NOW!

None of that is what you could actually experience now,

if you gave up this past/future thought system. The Ego lives and breathes in this past/future matrix.

So let's play a game. Here are the rules:

Look at that watch on your wrist, and for the next ten minutes, *pretend* there is no past or future (Your Ego will have to do the pretending because it believes in the past/future).

Every time you have the briefest of thoughts related to either the past or the future, don't try to change it or stop it. Just become aware of it and say to yourself (even if you don't believe it), "That thought about _____ is meaningless."

Do this as often as a past/future thought comes up (which will more than likely be constantly). After each thought just say, "That thought about _____ is meaningless."

Just notice your experience. Notice what you're thinking and feeling each time. I challenge you to do this for a whole day sometime. In that case, simply notice throughout the day when you seem to be thinking thoughts about the past/future and then say, "That thought about _____ is meaningless." You may be surprised what happens.

But back to your ten minute exercise. So what did you notice? Surprisingly, many people report that when they say "That thought about _____ is meaningless" there is an immediate and usually very brief sense of relief, quickly followed by intellectually questioning that experience of relief.

Other people experience an immediate sense of irritation (Still attached to that belief that your thoughts about the past/future have meaning, huh?).

If you experienced that brief sense of relief, it is because for a split second, you were in the NOW and had an opening of awareness.

You challenged your conventional Ego state that is completely wedded to the belief that thinking about past/present has some kind of value. The usual Ego state stopped working for a brief period, and the result was relief.

Either way, relief or irritation, try it for a day. Jump into the unknown, the unfamiliar, and unpracticed, even if it seems silly or untrue. See what happens. You may be very, very surprised.

After all, you're the one who wanted to read this book about *Undoing*. Nobody said it would be easy!

Chapter IV: And Yet, Another Chapter.

Are We More Than Our Thoughts, Emotions, Body Sensations, and Reactions?

Thoughts come and go creating a person in the world.
It is all an illusion.
We discover who we really are
when we stop imagining.

Self-concept. What a goofy word when we really look at it. We already have become aware that concepts, or constructs, are just a group of words around a central theme, there is no reality to a concept, and it's just a concept.

So we have this made up group of words that try and "define" (another thought process) something called the Self.

Of course the Self is just another group of words around a central theme. So we have a group of words around a group of words trying to define something we made up!

We have a construct that we are about to begin to *deconstruct*.

The Reader: The self is a very dense mat of thoughts, memories, interacting with powerful physical sensations that give the thoughts and memories a sense of physical reality. They are powerful in the body.

In talking with groups, one of my favorite requests is for individuals to "point to the Self". After a few minutes of blank stares and silence, people start pointing to their head, their chest area, their eyes, their body in general, the "third eye" (an area on the forehead just above and between the eyes), and various other places I won't mention here.

Sometimes when they see the person standing next to them pointing to some other place than the one they identified, they change their place to the one where the other person is pointing!

In the middle of this exercise I ask everyone to "freeze in place" and look around. What do they see? A whole group of people pointing to all kinds of places.

The Reader: This makes sense because feelings that thought precipitates are all over the body. The self feels it is contained in the body. Ask a group where they feel stress in their bodies – they will indicate places all over the body.

Another variation of this exercise is asking people to point to the Mind, or Heart, or Ego or "Place of Knowing". Once again, we find people pointing to all kinds of body parts.

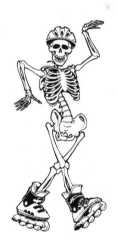

So what do we generally believe about these concepts (group of words)? We somehow believe that the Self (as well as the other concepts) is somehow within our bodies although we don't really know where.

Try this yourself. Stand in front of a mirror and ask yourself to point to, or place your finger on, where your Self is (or any of the other concepts). Once you locate the place ask yourself, "How do I know for certain that this place is where my _____ is?"

What you will find is that you do not know where these concepts are located within you because they aren't. They are just concepts. They have no reality except what your thoughts think about them.

You are for all intents and purposes, making them up! Hold on to this understanding for awhile as we explore further.

This possibly imaginary Self seems to be made up of thoughts and feelings about ourselves, others and our environment (the world). This imaginary Self which according to many people, seems to be living somewhere in our bodies, appears to be made up of thoughts and feelings.

The Reader: Are we even making "you" up? Seems

like a logically difficulty. How can there be a "you" to make you up?

If that might be the case, let's examine thoughts and feelings more carefully. To do this, let me ask you a few questions:

1. How many thoughts would you say you have from the moment you wake up until the moment you go to sleep every day? Five hundred? A Thousand? Ten Thousand? A Hundred Thousand? Maybe more?

2. Are thoughts constantly coming and going all day long?

3. Do you remember *all* the thoughts you had in the last twelve hours? How about the past hour? How about the last half hour? How about five minutes ago?

4. If you don't remember all these thoughts, where did they go?

5. The same question can be asked of emotions. If you're not having the identical emotion you had twelve hours ago, where did that emotion go?

6. Are YOU the thought or emotion you had twelve hours ago? How about an hour ago?

I think from this line of inquiry we can validly state that we are not the thoughts we have or the emotions we feel.

The Reader: Is the fact that we have thoughts and feelings that come and go, are transient, proof that we are our thoughts and feelings or evidence of the lack of reality of self? Isn't the self just thoughts and feelings and memories? Is there something else to it? People have argued for a long time that there is a soul – an essence that isn't thoughts. This is the thing they hope will go on after the body dies. The whole basis for duality lies in there being a self that observes everything else – that is separate from thoughts feelings. If we are not the thoughts and feelings we have then there is a duality between us and not us.

Thousands upon thousands of them come and go all day long. And when they go, we don't know where they go to. So logically the next question would be, if we are not our thoughts or our emotions which are constantly changing, coming and going all day long, then who are we?

If we are not this made up self construct, then who are we?

Obviously, we could not be aware that the thoughts and emotions we had twelve hours ago are not the same thoughts and feelings we are having right now, unless we were what we can call the *Observer* of our experience.

The *Observer* is not the specific experience, the *Observer* is aware of all these changing experiences.

We find the *Observer* is constant, the experiences are not. So we are not our thoughts and emotions, we are the *Observer* of thoughts and emotions that are coming and going, constantly changing.

We might also be aware that the *Observer* is not *experiencing* thoughts and emotions, but is simply *aware* of thoughts and emotions coming and going.

Thoughts and emotions seem to simply arise and dissipate within our Aware state of being.

The Reader: Are there separate observers? – Is there your observer and mine?

Earlier we looked at the generally accepted concept that "I" (my mind, thoughts, etc) am located in "my" body. We also believe that the body is who we are. That we are "in" our body. Another belief we have is that when we experience a sensation it has to be either good or bad, pleasant or unpleasant.

We decide what the sensation means to us.

There is now so much scientific literature that points to the understanding that pain is a *perception* that there is really no need to explain all of that in detail. Let's just look at a few obvious examples; phantom pain being one of the most significant.

There are many individuals who have lost a limb, yet continue to feel the sensation of pain in the limb that is no longer there. Clearly the particular body part is no longer experiencing pain sensations.

The perception of pain is not attached to that body part. We can look at an even simpler example. Two people can be in the same room with the same room temperature and one person may report feeling warmer while the other person reports feeling cooler.

Either sensation could be considered pleasant or unpleasant depending on the person's perception of the experience.

Let's play another imaginary game (although a somewhat gruesome one).

Let's pretend that for some reason your right leg just disappeared at the hip joint. Would you still be "you"?

What if both legs disappeared? What if both legs and both arms disappeared? Would you still be you? What if your entire lower body as well as both arms disappeared? Would you still be "you" then? What if your entire body below the neck disappeared? How about then? Would you still be you?

As you go on in this imaginary game, when does the sense of "you" disappear? You might see that it doesn't ever disappear.

This awareness of "you" in our imaginary game doesn't disappear even if your entire physical form goes away! (Hhmm.. I wonder if this explains what some people report as spirits?)

Let's try one more less gruesome game.

Get a physical sense of the skin outlining your entire body. Feel the sense of "you" contained within this skin. See if you can focus on this skin, feel it.

Now see if you can focus on the space surrounding this skin. See if you can feel this space around the edges of the skin.

Now we know that this skin (and everything within it) is only composed of atoms and molecules whirling around.

We also know that that space is also simply composed of atoms and molecules spinning around. So at this fundamental level, what's the difference in the atoms and molecules whirling around that we are calling skin and the atoms and molecules whirling around up against the skin in what we are calling space? In "reality" there is no difference at all.

The only difference has to do with our concepts and labels. We label that atoms and molecules whirling around within this thing we label as the skin as one thing, and the atoms and molecules whirling around outside this thing we label as the skin something else.

We label within the skin our "form" and the atoms and molecules "between" my form and another form as "space". They are simply made up distinctions between "this" and "that".

We create this duality and this sense of separateness which does not in actuality exist. I would like to suggest that, once again, that this whole labeling/separating structure is simply made up.

The Reader: By who, how?

Isn't it interesting that we see "space" as that which "separates" rather than that which "joins".

It is just as possible that this "space" between my form and your form is what joins us together, rather than what separates us.

Maybe there is only joining rather than separating. Maybe this whole perception of individual forms floating in all this space is an illusion (or delusion) in the first place.

A lot to consider! Talk to any Quantum Physicist and they would pretty much say the same thing.

Well, we have pretty much deconstructed the concept that we are our thoughts, emotions and body sensations; lets go for one more, our reactions. This is easy compared to the others. Can we have reactions that do not have thoughts, emotions, or body sensations involved?

I think not. And since we can see we are not our thoughts, emotions or body sensations, nor combinations of these things, who are we?

Since we are on a roll so to speak, and we still have to have these things we label as chapters in order to have a book, this is as good a time as any to end these thoughts and begin more thoughts on another page titled Chapter V.

Chapter V.

Who am I?

Every belief and assumption you have needs to be re-examined..
In this process you realize the
flaws in your perceptions.
You first begin by creating a "me"
which is followed by a
series of images you label as the
world, "other than me".
You define, label and separate all of your perceptions
every moment.
This is your great fictional story.

Now that we are hopefully starting to wonder if it could be possible that we really are not who we thought we were, and we seem to still be reading this thing called a book, we might be asking ourselves the more fundamental question, "Then, who am I?"

The problem with this question is not that it is asked, the problem might more be "Who is asking the question?"

Lets remember the Ego's agenda, "Inquiring minds want to KNOW". You might be thinking, "Oh no, are we back there again??! And Yes, we are.

Lets focus for a moment on the concept of "Being" rather than "Knowing". How many times have you heard, "Just Be", or "Be here now". What do these statements actually mean to you?

If we are in our Ego/doing/knowing state... they don't mean much, or they just sound ridiculous and irritate us. So just notice your reaction to these statements.

It will tell you a lot about who you perceive yourself to be. It's the old Zen, Taoist, Advaita Vedanta thing (those Ancient teachings had it right!). You can only know who you are in this present moment because that's who you are. YOU aren't the Doer, you're the Be'er. What does it feel like to be in this present moment since it's the only moment you can be in?

Do you quickly want to jump into the past or future? Do you want to immerse yourself in thought to escape now? How about spending "time" now labeling everything around you as good/bad, right/wrong?

How about going to sleep?

Do you want to do just about anything in an attempt to avoid now? Maybe it would be easier if someone just told me who I am?

That is easier. And there are plenty of people who will tell you who you are (sometimes for a hefty fee, but hey, it's only money).

The problem here is they don't know who you are. ONLY YOU can know who you are. The real question is "Do you really *want* to know who you are??"

Or are you good for now just perceiving yourself as a separate entity playing the Ego game of struggling to know yourself?

The Reader: I think we can't avoid that change doesn't happen to "me". Deepening awareness that we (several I's) are not who we thought, but who we really are." I think this is the problem of duality and not just semantics. I cannot become "that" perhaps "that" can clear up me.

So here's another game. You'll need some preplanning for this one. After you read about the game, you may just continue reading without taking time to actually play the game.

But I would like to suggest you take the time to actually play the game before you continue.

The goal of the game is to notice (be Aware) of what you experience while playing the game. That's it! Just notice what you are experiencing.

Just reading through the game is not the same as experiencing the game by playing it.

Preplanning:

Take two sheets of paper. On one sheet of paper list twenty "positive" things that define who you are. Start each line with "I am a _____". For instance, I am a good business person, I am a good father, I am a spiritual person, etc...

After you have written down your 20 definitions of who you are, take time to read each of them again, and as you read each one, look at the images that come to mind, the associations with the definition.

Then take the second piece of paper and write down twenty "negative" things that define who you are using the same format, "I am a _____". For example, I am a terrible speaker, I am fat, I am too suspicious of others, etc.. Don't be shy; certainly you can identify twenty negative definitions.

Now take a pair of scissors and cut the paper so that you have forty small slips of paper with one definition on each slip. I know that's a lot of writing and cutting, but you need to have a lot of definitions for this experience to be real to you.

One you have your forty slips of paper mix them up all together in something. It can be anything. For those of you who like ritual you can put them into something meaningful.

Now find a quiet place where you won't be disturbed for awhile. If you are a meditator, do whatever you usually do to be in a meditative state. For non-meditators, just sit quietly, take a few breaths, and close you eyes.

Place the container with all the forty slips of paper in front of you.

Now in this quiet state, pick one piece of paper out of whatever you have it in. Open your eyes briefly. Read the statement, and then close you eyes, crumple the piece of paper up and say, "but I am not that!" Notice how you feel.

Do this process in this exact same way, for each statement, positive or negative, and notice how you feel after crumpling it up and saying, "but I am not that!"

Here are some things you may experience:

1. Nothing

2. Resistance at first to saying "but I am not that!" when crumpling up the positive statements.

3. A sense of relief at first when saying "I am not that" when crumpling up the negative statements.

4. As the process continues... a sense of confusion, not being able to differentiate the positive statements from the negative statements after awhile.

5. A sense of calmness after the confusion.

6. At times, a feeling of just wanting to stop and not continue with the process.

7. Possibly the awareness arises that you really aren't these things.

So, just take some time to "debrief" after the experience. What did it feel like to challenge the Ego sense of who you are? The Ego identifies with roles (positive or negative).

What did it feel like to dis-identify with these definitions of who you think you are? Did you notice that when you dis-identified with the positive definitions of who you were it required dis-identifying with your whole perceived history (your story) related to that specific definition?

Did you notice that even when you dis-identified with the negative definitions of who you were, in the background, there was a sense of loss?

Did you notice the whole exercise brought up feelings of loss and grief? This exercise symbolically represents death to the Ego, giving up, losing your perceived Ego identity, the story of who you are.

Did you recognize, even for a moment, who you really are when you let go of your story?

If you experienced nothing, that doesn't mean you didn't play the game correctly.

What did experiencing nothing mean to you?

Can you really experience nothing?

And finally, who was the you who was aware of having all these experiences? (Are you experiencing "being *Undone*" yet?).

If not, no big deal... there's a lot more coming...

The Ego really isn't very smart. Remember its only goal is continuation for better or worse. So it likes processes, thing to do, things to achieve.

So we play with it, we use it to Undo itself. It doesn't realize it's undoing itself because it's too caught up in doing the process.

Reader: So maybe we don't have to take this Ego thing so seriously?

So let's humor the Ego and develop a process that undoes it. There really is no process but the Ego doesn't know that. In the following chapter we will set up a more formal process to assist the Ego in undoing itself. Won't that be fun! This is a serious subject so you have to find the humor in it somewhere!

Reader: I never thought of considering this as a game. How freeing!

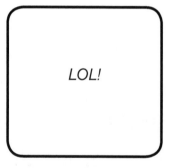

Chapter VI: The Following Chapter.

A Process for Undoing.

Sleeping is much more comfortable
that the work it takes to
wake up.
Most seekers of the truth prefer to
settle for improving their
existing stories.
Seeing clearly is obtained by living behind the mind.

For those who are still determined to KNOW, this will make you feel better.

Now the most important part of this process is to do it regardless of how you feel about it, and regardless whether or not you think the statements are true. You don't have to believe the statements, just say them and then let the idea sink in.

You might just want to stick to one statement for a day or two. See how you feel and what you experience cumulatively. Wherever the words "I' or 'You" are used, they generally refer to the Ego state of consciousness.

1. "I" don't really know the "purpose" of anything.

I have all kinds of beliefs and opinions about the purpose of things, but I don't *really know* the ultimate purpose of anything!

What does this statement mean? Well, the Ego (limited perception) is finite and bound by time (thoughts based on past/present/future). It can only know things based on its limited perception of reality. It thinks it knows the purpose of everything!

But because it can only see reality through it's limited perception and cannot see the whole, it couldn't possibly really know the ultimate purpose of anything. You don't really know the purpose of "that bird" or "that house" or "that flower"

This may feel very confusing when you repeat this statement frequently. And you may notice the Ego resistance as you say it. "Of course I know the purpose of things!" But the "I" is the Ego speaking.

Reader; Wow, this really means giving up this knowing thing I've been doing all my life!

2. "I" do not 'see' anything as it really is. Everything I see with my eyes are simply thoughts about the past.

We touched on this in earlier chapters when we examined thoughts and the Ego. When we look at something, no matter what it is, we have a *thought* about it.

We have seen that thoughts are simply something that we create and are primarily based on" past" associations. Remember the ceramic jug example?

When I look at my dog, Clifford the Cock-a Poo, I see a form. I "remember" that this form is something I call a word, Clifford.

I then remember that this form did this or that yesterday. The only way I know this form is called a "dog", is by my current thoughts about what a dog is based on associations from the past.

When we say we "remember" we are simply saying that my *current* thought is based on a past association (a thought about the past).

This is why we never see a form now as it really is. This is also why we hold on to past judgments about people even if that person is different now. The Ego really wants to hold on to past thoughts.

Reader: So I really don't see anything as new or fresh. It's just old rehashed perceptions. Now I get the Buddhist concept of "Beginners Mind", seeing things without the idea that it is something I already know.

Past thoughts give meaning to the Ego. These thoughts are then projected into the future. In this way the Ego believes nothing ever really changes and it can continue to exist. We can see this is a misperception based on the Ego need for security.

If we are able to see something as it really is, we would have no "knowledge" (past associations) of it. It would simply be what it is, and we would not be able to label it, judge it, or be separate from it.

It would just be a "happening" happening now.

"You" would be Aware. You would be in the present moment experiencing Now as it really is. You might experience awe, a feeling of bliss, a sense of Oneness. You might feel terrified!

3. "My" thoughts are meaningless

This is usually a difficult one. We might be able to live with *some* of my thoughts are meaningless but *all* of my thoughts!! To distinguish between some meaningless thoughts and some meaningful thoughts we would have to first continue to believe that we know the purpose of things (including our thoughts), and that we can see things as they really are now (which we can't).

We know that "current" thoughts are based on the past and future which do not exist now. We know at a deeper level that we really do not know the purpose of things.

And we know that the Ego is based on the belief that past and future thoughts have meaning.

We also are getting an inkling that thoughts are simply

something we create and have no external meaning at all except for the meaning we give them.

Consider how much time you have spent (pretty much constantly) trying to judge what is meaningless and meaningful, what is good or bad, what is right or wrong, what is" worth it" and what is" not worth it".

Exhausting, isn't it?

Reader: Oh my poor mind!!

This is simply the pastime of the Ego. It has to stay very busy and appear necessary or it won't be needed.

The *Reader: What has caused humans to invest in self related thought so much? Is it just a pastime?*

Also think about all the times that what you judged "in the present" and labeled as negative, meaningless, bad, wrong, worthless, etc... turned out to be the opposite in the long run.

The Reader: And would the opposite even be meaningful, good right, worthwhile – did they turn out in our judgment to be positive?

If you really spend some time doing this you will be

amazed at how much of the time you spent on a relatively worthless preoccupation of the mind.

This may help you to more fully realize that your thoughts are meaningless. If you don't think this is true, that is just another meaningless thought! (It just never ends, does it?)

4. I am aware that there is "some state" that is more than "me", this Ego state.

Call it anything you like or call it nothing-at-all. It doesn't really matter at all what you label "It". Even the label "It" doesn't define "It" because "It" can't be defined.

Remember only the Ego state labels, defines, puts things into little boxes. Throughout history people have attempted to define "It". A few examples are:

The Ground of Being, Awareness, Emptiness, The Unborn, GOD, gods and goddesses, The Father, the Mother, The Universal Mind, Consciousness, Pure Consciousness, THAT which IS, Non-Being, Brahman, The Buddha Mind, Nothing, The Way, The Stillness, What Is, Love, and about four thousand other words.

Reader: I'm really glad I don't have to keep trying to figure out what "It" is because I can't.

That's the thing. They're all just WORDS! Now you may have a particular affinity (or aversion) to any of these words based on your thoughts and associations, but who cares! Remember, thoughts and associations are created by the Ego.

The Reader: What is the alternative to thought?.

Throughout history many ways to KNOW "It" have been designed and apparently, according to some, some of the many ways have worked for some, but apparently not all.

To avoid the Ego trap of labeling, judging and defining, we could look at this "It" another way. "It' is all of the above. That's it! Do we really have to pick and choose among diverse terms , ways, processes, paths, approaches?

That all sounds like Ego tasks to me. Personally I like to call "It" Sylvia, but that's just me.

In any event, we are aware that our limited Ego state does not, and cannot make us happy. It's always based on winning and losing, struggling.

One of the Buddhist terms for this Ego state is "The Monkey Mind". Always chattering about, swinging from tree limb to tree limb, carrying on LOUDLY, and basically just going around in circles.

So if we can be Aware of this Monkey Mind, who is it that is being Aware? This Aware state certainly seems "bigger, "deeper", "more expansive" and much less freaked out than our Ego state.

Could this be the "It"?

Reader" "It" can't really be that simple, can it?

For those who are not Aware of this type of "It", I highly recommend beginning Insight Meditation practice, or some other form of Awareness practice. It can be the beginning of Undoing. Almost any type of Altered State or NOC (Non Ordinary Consciousness) experience can begin the Undoing.

I find these terms *Altered State* and *Non Ordinary Consciousness* to be interesting concepts. It implies that our usual day-to-day state or non-altered state is the "ordinary" state and than anything else is an "altered" state.

I would like to suggest an alternative definition (remember they're all just concepts). Could it be that our *Ordinary State* is actually the "It", but our Ego spends so much time creating an altered state that we call our usual day-to-day experience, that we actually believe this altered state of usual experience is what is real?

This is a major point. Try reading it again slowly and let "It" speak to you. A lot to consider here.

So let's play another game (I know you just love these games!)

Reader: No, I really don't! Although, I see that the

"games" seem to get at "it" when words by themselves don't seem to be able to do that.

Imagine for a moment that you are the "It" and the "It" is just playing a game itself. Imagine that the "It" just likes to create stories; illusions, to keep from being bored. The illusion it is creating right now is called the *The Story of You!*

Now just like any good book (except this one), a story has to have a beginning, a middle, and an end, otherwise it wouldn't be an interesting story.

And when we read good stories we like to have some drama in there, there needs to be the Hero, and in order to have a Hero there has to be one or more villains for the Hero to overcome and defeat.

And of course the Hero has to have a group of people who see him or her as the Hero, and the villains have to have a group of people on his or her side to fight the Hero.

Now the story wouldn't be very exciting and keep our attention if the Hero didn't have to go through trials and tribulations, almost losing the battle, only to eventually come out victorious at the end of the story.

So in this current story of "You" all these aspects needs to be in play, otherwise you're kind of boring. All of the "bad things" that *seem to happen to you* would need to be in the story so that you would have things to overcome and be victorious at the end.

Remember the story has to be *really dramatic* to be interesting, so you will have to almost lose to the villains frequently and then with superhuman strength, overcome them.

So you need those villains in the story, sometimes lots of them; a roving herd of marauders, an evil king or queen, all kinds of tests and trials to overcome. Sounds exciting doesn't it?

The good thing about stories is that we know they are stories. We can simply stop reading or listening to the story if we become bored, if it becomes too frightening, if it's not turning out the way we want it to.

Well, you created the *Story of You*!

It's just a story, a fairy tale, an illusion. Sometimes fun, sometimes not so fun.

You're creating it every minute.

Ever thought about just putting the *Story of You* down for awhile? Just turning the book face down on the coffee table? Maybe just putting it back on the book shelf with all the other stories?

There are billions of stories on that bookshelf, yours isn't that unique. Remember they all end the same way.

So with the *Story of You* back on the book shelf, who are you, if you're not this fictional story?

Reader: My mind is fried! And I'm thinking that's a good thing!!

Another option is to continue the story, but remember

you are *all of the characters* in the story. Maybe the *Story of You* will be more entertaining to you that way. It's just your story, play it any way you want to.

It doesn't really make any difference in the long run, it's just an illusion. All stories end the same way anyway.

By the way, you can even have a definable *God* in your story if it helps. But be careful with that one. Once you bring "It" into your story, it may not just be *your* story anymore and you may not want to put it back on the bookshelf ever again.

5. "My senses are unreliable. I cannot determine who I am, or what the world really is, through my senses."

Have you ever watched the television show called the Fear Factor? It's a great example of the statement above. If you haven't watched the show, they put people in a completely darkened room but you can see them on the screen because they use some kind of night vision cameras to tape it.

So here is this individual in the completely darkened room and they tell them to move around and experience things. One of my favorites was when they had this guy reach into a tank that had water in it. In the water was one of those long Italian two or three foot salamis (nice and greasy) and some other similarly gross stuff.

So he had to reach into this tank, having absolutely no idea what was in the tank (and assuming it wasn't something "good" I suppose) and use his available senses, in this case touch, to determine what it was. Before he even moved his hand into the tank he started screaming (now this happened to be a big burly jock type guy, not that that makes any difference).

Can you imagine all of the thoughts he was creating about what might be in the tank even before he touched anything?

Very tentatively, and screaming the entire time, his fingers first touched the water. He jerked his hand back from the water and screamed even louder, contorting his body, visibly shaking. Now remember so far all he touched was water.

But of course, he had to continue. So hand, visibly shaking, back into the water. Now the salami was patiently waiting at the bottom of the tank. Seconds felt like centuries.

Imagine as he slowly moved his hand down in the tank not feeling anything tangible for awhile (I was concerned he was either going to have a heart attack or at least wet his pants). Every inch down into the tank he was screaming louder.

Finally, the tip of one finger touched the top of the sausage. You would have thought he had just touched pure Evil! He jerked his hand out of the water, still screaming, and lunged away from the tank to where, I suppose, he thought the door to the room might be. Remember he could see *absolutely nothing*. As he stumbled around in this empty space of darkness he apparently became even more freaked out (I didn't think he could possibly scream louder, but he surprised me. He could!).

Eventually somehow he was saved from his own thoughts, although I forget how. I think he eventually bumped into a team mate in the room who also stumbling around, and after freaking out about touching "something else" he realized it was a team mate and calmed down (apparently terror loves company).

I am guessing as you read this story, you also started to feel some of the same feelings he was feeling to a lesser degree (I hope).

I can't think of an example that more clearly and *experientially* reveals to you that our thoughts and our senses are not reliable indicators of "reality".

Notice that while you were just thinking about what I described in the story you began to feel some of the characters feelings (terror isn't fun, is it?) even though you intellectually *knew* ahead of time that there was just a sausage in the tank!

It's pretty clear that even when you know something intellectually, it doesn't mean you won't create all kinds of fantasies (scary or otherwise) that are not related at all to the "facts".

The Reader: What's afraid, and what's it afraid of? Is it the senses that are unreliable or the observer that is processing the information being fed by the senses? An unreliable observer?

Also notice the burly guy could not depend on sight as a reliable witness, and obviously he could not depend on his sense of touch.

What about the sense of hearing? Now we know that's unreliable. How many times do we regularly hear a sound, imagine what it is, and shortly find out that isn't what it was at all. That happens (to most of us) all the time.

My favorite example of the unreliability of sight comes from the philosophical/spiritual path of Advaita Vedanta. The example given is as follows:

A young man sees a coiled snake across the field. In that particular region, there were many poisonous snakes which generally were not fearful objects unless it was coiled and ready to strike. He saw a young woman, a stranger, walking through the field toward, but apparently unaware of, the coiled snake.

She was much closer to the snake than he, but not yet within striking distance, and he was very concerned for her welfare.

His terror mounted as he could see the horror about to unfold, so he yelled loudly while running full steam in her direction waving his hands in all directions.

The young woman saw this yelling, waving, running stranger headed directly toward her, reached into her skirt, pulled out a dagger she kept for protection, and quickly hurled the knife at this approaching danger.

The dagger lodged in the young man's heart and instantly killed him. He fell to the ground.

The young woman, after composing herself, felt relieved that she had avoided this dangerous enemy, and resumed her path toward the *rope* she had coiled and left in the field. So we see here a young man whose *visual* misperception of reality cost him his life.

Look at the entire fantasy, although unintentional, that he created by misperceiving what was really there, along with mentally seeing a terrible outcome for the young lady that he hoped to prevent.

Look at the very strong emotions he created with the fantasy.

Alas, the young woman also visually misinterprets the reality of the situation. She sees a form (the young man) racing toward her screaming and waving his arms, and creates a thought fantasy that he is some deranged person coming to do her harm rather than someone who is coming to save her.

We would probably have that same interpretation under those circumstances. Remember she knew that the coiled rope was not a snake in the first place.

I would like to suggest that we frequently misinterpret the "reality" of the situation because it is filtered through our very unreliable senses (sight, hearing, touching, tasting and smelling).

Hopefully with a less dramatic outcome than the figures in the story above, but... we do it all the time.

Just think back to all the times you thought you saw something, but when you examined it more closely, it wasn't what you thought it was.

Think of the times that you began to taste something (something that you expected to taste similarly to something you had eaten before) and to your disgust (or maybe delight) it didn't taste the way you expected it to at all.

Think of the times you thought you heard something, or thought what you heard was something, only to find out that what you heard wasn't what it was at all (The old "Was that gun fire or a car backfiring?" applies here.).

We already have an example from the Fear Factor about how touch can be, shall we say, misleading to say the least.

And we know that smelling is completely reliable, right?? Nope.

I am thinking about another television related example. In this case it is a commercial for some air freshener. The commercial involves two individuals sitting in a clearly smelly room with a large garbage can with obviously smelly stuff under their noses.

They are blindfolded, and on top of the trash can is the miraculous air freshener. When asked where they think they are, they say things like "in a meadow", "in a garden surrounded by flowers"… etc..

Now of course we know they are actors paid to say that. and even if the place smelled like cat s - - - t, they would still be sighing deeply and contentedly and saying they were in a garden surrounded by flowers, but it does prove a point.

The sense of smell can be very unreliable. Again, think of your own examples, hopefully not one involving cat s- - t.

An easy one would be coming into a house where someone was cooking and you remark, "Wow that broiled Salmon smells great! When do we eat?" (Well, maybe this is an example about cat s- - t).

The host or hostess looks at you, clearly irritated that you "got it wrong" and tells you, "We are having baked chicken!"

Now you've really got a problem. So what's in that house that smells like dead burned fish? Your host/ hostess is now aware you smell something fishy!

I think my suggestion that we frequently misinterpret the reality of the situation as interpreted through our senses has been made. I think we can see that relying on our senses to speak to what is true, or who I am, is a less than secure position.

Out of all of these sensory misperceptions of who we are, I am guessing that the sense of sight is our biggest downfall.

We have this very deep *belief* (a group of thoughts strung together into what appears to be something true) that what we see with our eyes is accurate and therefore real! How unfortunate, and I would suggest, incorrect.

This is a check in. So, are you *Undone* yet? Partially *Undone*? Confused and bordering on psychosis (or boredom) at this point? Experiencing overwhelming and gut wrenching Existential anxiety? Great! You're on the path!

(A reminder that nowhere in this book did I guarantee that by reading it, or should I say, by "doing it", that you would experience eternal bliss and supreme happiness. If that's what you're looking for, find a Guru, and good luck with that. Let me know how it turns out.)

So, take a deep breathe, or rouse yourself from slumber, and let's continue....

6. There is nothing I need to do, or can do, to experience "It".

Ah, don't we hate to hear this when somebody says it? Unfortunately, like so many things that really are true, we hate to hear it.

Reader: I want to be able to DO something!!!!

First of all, "It" is not something *we experience*; it is something that *experiences us*! Now that's a mouthful to digest, isn't it? So what the hell does that mean?

For a feeble attempt at an explanation, I turn once again to the Advaita Vedanta tradition. The imagery used here is the wave and the ocean.

A reminder that words and images cannot possibly define or explain something that is more, bigger, greater than words and images. So words, images, and concepts can only be used as *pointers.*

Pointers simply point to, or suggest, that which cannot be explained by words, images and concepts. Pointers are not "It".

So back to the Advaita Vedanta image (pointer) of the wave and the ocean.

We have all seen an ocean at some point in our lives.

What we notice is that the ocean simply moves. When it moves in particular ways, waves are created, some big, some little, some deadly (Tsunami's), some gently flowing, some cresting at great heights.

When we see a wave, what do we call it? Of course, we call it a wave. But why? Why have we separated one movement of the ocean and called it something other than the ocean?

Well, we do that because we like to break things down in parts and label them. It's just fun! However, it serves no real purpose.

When we hear on the news that large waves are beating down one coastline or another, why don't we just say the ocean is beating down the coastline? Ever thought about that? It's similar to what we do with clouds, and trees, and just about everything, but that example will be given later.

So back to our wave "on" the ocean again. Now in actuality the wave isn't "on" the ocean, the wave IS the ocean, but we really do like to separate things, and then spend time giving the separated things (parts of the whole) a meaning of its own.

As we watch a wave "on" the ocean, we give meaning to it. The wave appears to have a function all its own. It is supposed to do certain things like build up and then decrease, or whatever waves do.

The wave begins to take on a personality of its own. It "gently laps", it "flows", it "crests", it "builds", it "ebbs", it "shimmers"; it just does an amazing number of things. The only problem is, it doesn't exist!

We have taken a whole (the ocean), arbitrarily separated one of its many movements, named it something else (a wave), given it a separate meaning, described it, and determined its functions, but in Reality, it's just the ocean doing it's thing, pretty much undisturbed and unaware of the "wave" since it isn't anything.

The ocean (the whole) just keeps on rolling along being

the whole. We have not really affected the ocean at all but calling one if its movements a wave, have we.

So here's the point. The Whole is completely unaffected, and unaware, that we have arbitrarily, in our minds, separated it into parts, because it is not parts, it is the whole.

This separation thing is just our amusing pastime, our mental game, our determination to see separateness that is not really there.

Unfortunately for us, this amusing pastime makes us miserable in the long run, and it's completely made up by us! A figment of our overly active imagination, an illusion.

Are you getting "It" now? Maybe you already got "It". If not, don't despair, there's still time. There's actually all the time in the world because that concept is an illusion too. But wait, I move too fast. There are more chapters to come.

So now let's apply the wave and ocean analogy to our Selves. It's pretty easy to do. We actually think we are the illusion known as the wave! We think we have a separate reality from the ocean (*The Whole,* or *Pure Consciousness* is the word we can use for the time being).

Again it doesn't matter what word we use because the word is not "It." We think we move independently from the whole. We think we are a separate entity from the whole.

We think we have a beginning (wave forming) known as birth, a middle (wave cresting) known as now, and an end (wave decreasing) known as death.

So as long as we are determined to hold on to the Ego illusion that we are a separate form (the wave), sooner or later we will end as the wave, won't we.

Now just because the wave has created the illusion that it is separate, there is no factual evidence at all that it is separate.

As the matter of fact, if we remove the labeling, the fact is, it is not a separate entity at all (regardless of what the wave may choose to believe).

And even if the wave does choose to believe this illusion, that belief has no affect on the ocean. The ocean knows the wave is not separate from it.

Maybe the ocean just humors the wave while it's playing this separation game because, in the long run, it knows it doesn't make any difference what the wave believes.

Looking at it through this analogy, the wave really *believes* it has substance, form, a reason for being, a purpose, a beginning and an end, and that it is "in control" of it's individual movements, but we can see from the oceans perspective, the wave believing all this is really pretty silly.

Our statement earlier was, *There is nothing "I" need to do, or can do, to experience "It"*. If we now see the "I" as the wave, and "It" as the ocean, it makes complete sense why there is nothing "You" need to do, or can do, to experience "It" because you already are "It".

Reader: You mean I'm "God"? I'm "It"? Mind blower.

There is nothing the wave needs to do, or can do to experience itself as the ocean because it already IS the ocean. It was just confused about its identity.

By the way, confusion about your identity has been diagnosed as a psychiatric disorder by the American Psychiatric Association, so you better get this cleared up fast!

Remember the wave believes it has a separate purpose and function apart from the ocean, that purpose and function is to be a wave.

I'm thinking all the wave can "do" is to do nothing more than realize the misperception of itself, to realize it has no power of its own (I believe this is called *surrender* and *spiritual humility* in some circles).

The question for the wave would be, when does it want to recognize, become Aware of, this because sooner or later, with the wave doing absolutely nothing, it will be realized. It's only a matter of "wave time".

I think if you stick with this analogy for awhile, you will definitely get "It".

But I could be wrong. After all, I don't know the purpose of anything, remember!

Now let's look at one more example from Advaita Vedanta. Similarly as simple and complex as the wave-ocean analogy.

There is a sky, or so it appears. Within this sky there are clouds and it appears that different clouds have different shapes, different "bodies" so to speak.

We say this cloud looks like this, and that cloud looks like that. Some clouds appear darker than others. Our vision tells us each cloud we see is different and separate from the others.

Of course, if we watch the cloud it is always changing "form". Clouds appear then disappear. One cloud that looks like this begins to look like that. These clouds are constantly changing within what we call the sky.

When a cloud disappears, where does it go? It changes form and is once again just the sky.

Advaita teaches us that we are like the clouds. We think we have a distinct "form" but the form is actually constantly changing, it is not solid as we imagine, just as the cloud is not solid.

We (apparent solid forms) exist within the sky and are really just part of the sky. The clouds apparent separateness is in actually nonexistent. The cloud IS the sky.

All that separates the cloud from the sky is our less than reliable seeing sense, and our labeling one part of the whole as separate from the whole. Clouds are an illusion, just as we as separate forms are an illusion.

The cloud can do nothing to be the sky, it already IS the sky. It may think (as clouds oftentimes do) that it is separate from the sky, but that is just a thought of separateness, it is not its reality.

So the sky just waits patiently as the form assumes a separate identity until it dissipates and is once again the sky. The sky has all the time in the world; it already is Aware of the truth. It simply observes the cloud thinking it's a cloud.

A reminder that a "cloud" is nothing except the definition we have given something that appears to be real.

7. " I" am not a victim of the world "I" see. My own thoughts of separation and attack make me the victim.

Let's recap so we can better understand this one.

The Ego is all about separation. The best way to be separate is to see "Me" and "them". "Me" is good, "them" are bad. The "bad" attack the "good" somehow or they couldn't be labeled as "Bad".

Remember the Ego is all about feeling secure, but believes there is a lack of resources.

So the Ego has to protect itself from those who would steal its security. "Them" are competitors who would attack "Me" in a split second.

For the Ego to exist, it HAS to believe it is currently being attacked by "them", or it will be attacked shortly. So the strategy is to be the first to attack! Cut them off at the knees! Annihilate then before they can annihilate you!

In your small little mind you create World War III. This world war is occurring in your significant other relationship, in your family, at work, with the old lady down the street! EVERYWHERE, because it is in your mind!

You are the attacker AND the attackee. The aggressor and the victim. The hero and the enemy.

Reader: I'm realizing I ALWAYS live in attack thoughts one way or another. That IS my reality!

Unfortunately, Egos frequently (if not constantly) share this attack delusion. Just look around you. Everyone is attacking everyone else one way or another. We can even attack nicely or under the guise of helping.

Let's look at some examples.

"Surely, you didn't really mean what you just said?? Only someone with an IQ of 10 would say something like that, and I know you're really smart, so you couldn't have really meant that"

That is a thinly guised attack thought. What you really meant was, "You idiot! How dare you say that to me! Now I'll get you and make you feel really stupid!"

That's right! Cut em off at the knees!

How about this one. "Why, you look so tired and exhausted! You know, you really should take better care of yourself".

Why don't you just say, "Listen fool! You take lousy care of yourself and that's why you feel so tired and exhausted. It's your own fault!"

That attack thought should really make them feel better, don't you think?

My favorite one liner is "Here, let me help you!"

Of course, what you're really saying is, "Obviously you can't, or don't know how to do this the right way, I do! So I'll do it for you. I'm so much better at this than you are!"

The Ego loves to feel smarter, better, more equipped, healthier, quicker, etc... and it will find others to be sure it proves it.

I have always found attack thoughts to be most prevalent, and obvious to those who know about attack thoughts, in the significant other (or parent/child) relationship.

Look at all the times you have attacked your spouse or child, or co-worker. Even if you didn't verbally say it, you were thinking it. And either way, you are creating separation in your mind. It doesn't really matter if you EVER express it verbally; you are still creating separation through attack.

It's all in your head!

Now of course the Ego doesn't really care who or what it attacks, or who it sees as attacking it, as long as there is attack.

We even set ourselves up to be attacked, verbally, and possibly physically!

You think not? How many times have you egged

someone on until they lost it emotionally and verbally (hopefully not physically).

You know exactly what buttons to push.. and you consistently push them! Come on, be honest with yourself.

As stated earlier, the Ego doesn't care who or what it attacks as long as it attacks. Unfortunately, one of it's favorite pastimes is attacking itself (YOU!).

We don't really need examples to make this clearer, do we? Just look at what you do to your "self" constantly! (And I do mean CONSTANTLY.)

Reader: Self hate, low self esteem, guilt, failure, it never stops! AARRGGHH!

The good news out of this never ending horror is that we can become AWARE. We can become Aware that attack thoughts, just like all our other thoughts, are meaningless.

The *only purpose* of these meaningless attack thoughts is to create the ILLUSION of separation.

Ever heard the saying," Do you want to be right, or do you want to be happy?" Think about it...alot!

8. "I can choose to see Love instead of Fear."

An amazing man, a psychiatrist named Gerald Jampolsky, wrote an amazing book called *"Love is Letting Go of Fear"*. If you haven't read it, go right to the bookstore (or you Kindle) and get it (after you finish this one first of course).

His concept is universal; there are ONLY two emotions, Love and Fear. What is not perceived as loving is a call for help. An individual is either loving in the moment, or fearful and calling for love.

Talk about a way to break right through that separation thing! If we are extending, or receiving, love we cannot feel separate.

Who was that guy...uummhh.. I remember his name from way back...he was a Guru or something...oh yeah, Jesus Christ. Didn't he say something about loving your enemies?

Well now, who in their right mind is going to choose to love their enemies?? The enemy did terrible things to me/us. I/we are good, and they are bad, bad, bad.

Don't you think us good guys should just shoot them or blow them up! Seems like the only right and just thing to do, don't you agree?

That'll fix THEM !

I think we can see that continuing to believe those attack thoughts are real will ultimately destroy all forms that exist. It's just a matter of time if we keep those thoughts up!

Let's imagine a different scenario. What if we actually did what that Guru said. What if we really did begin to see everyone, including ourselves, as either loving, or fearful and calling for love?

Would we perceive reality differently? Would we perceive our significant others, children, parents, co-workers, the old lady down the street differently? But more fundamentally, would we begin to perceive OURSELVES differently?

Might we actually begin to live in that One-ness, that Whole-ness, that our Ego clearly is not?

Dunno...but it certainly sounds like it would be worth it to try!

Reader: I am all for this! There doesn't really seem to

be any other option unless I want to just continue to be miserable.

9. "I can choose the perception of reality that is True."

I do have the choice to perceive things differently. The ONLY choice we really do have is perceive things differently. We can realize that our usual and initial perception of ourselves, and the world around us, is based on Ego perception.

And we now know that the Ego is only interested in attack thoughts, separation, the illusion of security, and believing that thoughts about the past and future are real.

We can assume that our initial thoughts and reactions to whatever we encounter (unpleasant or pleasant) will be this Ego perception. So it becomes easier to immediately withdraw from our initial experience, even if it seems "real" (logical, justified, the "truth") knowing that it is not.

Remember that "my" (Ego) thoughts are meaningless and "I" do not know the purpose of anything!

Simply the act of "stepping back" from our initial experience allows the possibility of Awareness to enter. Oftentimes when Awareness enters we realize a number of things.

One thing we may realize is that we do not have to do anything! We don't have to fix the experience, change it, control it, analyze it, attack it, hold on to it, or have any particular feeling about it. The experience just is!

We may also realize that the experience just arose, among the hundreds of other experiences we have.

It doesn't have to be personal; it doesn't have to MEAN anything! Whatever meaning the experience does/did have, we gave it with our thoughts. And we know our thoughts are meaningless, and we don't know the purpose of anything.

If we labeled the experience as painful, joyful, sad, or depressing (or anything else) we can simply become

Aware that we are labeling something that simply arose.

While we are busy labeling we are not Aware. We can also remember that 'I" collect experiences to add to "my story", and that my story is simply made up by me!

The *Dreamer* and the *Dream*:

One way of becoming Aware of this choice in perception, is the story of the Dreamer and the Dream.

Let's say I had a dream last night while I was sleeping. As I fell asleep, all of a sudden, with no warning, I began to be rudely pulled by unseen hands through what was apparently a hole in the sky, down, down, down, sinking into a very dark place.

I landed on the ground in this dark place. I was aware

there was danger all around me; big, bad, and ugly danger everywhere.

I knew I was going to have to fight to get out of this alive. Even people I vaguely recognized as "friends" were not. They were these monsters appearing as friends. Everyone was the enemy. I'm thinking I'm a goner for sure!

I saw lying on the ground in front of a long "magical" coat that was covered in barbed wire and spikes. I figured if I put this magical coat on none of the monsters could get me.

It seemed to be working; the only problem was as I stealthily maneuvered through this dark place avoiding monsters, the coat seemed to be getting heavier and heavier. Man that was one heavy coat! And it was getting heavier each minute. It began to really drag me down.

I could hardly take one step without feeling immobilized, but I keep struggling to take a step. I figured that if I stopped moving, I would just be "bird feed' for these monsters that were constantly surrounding me wherever I went.

I just couldn't get away from them. It seemed like when I was able to maneuver away from one, there would be two or three more blocking my way. I didn't know where I was going, but I sure didn't want to stay where I was!

This wasn't working out to well and I was exhausted, defeated, and terrorized. I was going downhill fast!

Soon I just couldn't take another step and fell in a terrorized heap on the ground. Now the coat seemed to be so heavy it was smothering me. I couldn't breathe, and somehow the barbed wire and spikes had worked their way through the coat and were piercing my skin.

Why the hell did I put this coat on in the first place??? Soon, the monsters gathered around me and began to claw at me, their huge teeth only a hairs breath from my skin, this was it! I'm done for!

Then just as quickly as the dream began, it ended. To my great relief, I was back in my warm cozy bed, completely unharmed, and I lived to tell this story!

Reader: You and I must be in the same head. I have dreams like that all the time.

This dream is one way of symbolically describing Awareness and the Ego experience. So let's unravel it a bit. Remember our imagery of the wave and the ocean? It's similar, except in this story the wave is having a really, really, really, bad time being a wave!

So here's the concept. We are both the Dreamer and the

Dream! The me who is awake prior to falling asleep is the Awake state (non Ego state) aware of the true reality. However, once I fall asleep I become the Dreamer (Ego state) who is dreaming the dream.

Now while I am dreaming, I don't realize I am simply having a dream and playing a part in the dream. The "Dreamer me" actually believes all those horrible things are happening in "real time".

I (the Dreamer) don't know I am CREATING the entire thing, including all the monsters. They seem very, very real to me at the time. Imagine if someone said to the Dreamer, "Hey chill, this is only a dream. Nothing bad can really happen to you".

More than likely the Dreamer would be yelling over his shoulder to that person, "Oh Yeah? Tell that to the monsters who are about to devour me!!"

That's the catch. The Dreamer doesn't know it's a dream and doesn't believe it! His experience is telling him those are real monsters with real teeth, and he's losing ground fast!

Now, when the dreamer suddenly wakes up from the dream, he almost immediately realizes it was a dream, and can now see, much to his relief, that everything he experienced in the dream, which was so real to him seconds ago, wasn't real at all.

Deep Awareness is much like waking up from a dream. A dream you really, really, really thought was true.

In our dream above, notice that the Dreamer, "me", created a coat (attack thoughts) to protect him (get security) from the monsters (the attackers in our thoughts). The only trouble with the coat is that it became very heavy, burdensome, and in the end was his downfall (attack thoughts are like that, they are our downfall in our Ego dream of reality).

Now the cool part is that in the dream, no matter how attacked the dreamer thought he was, he really wasn't at all!

Of course, in our day to day experience which we are calling reality, most of the time we are not aware that it is a dream. We hold on to the dream and believe it at all costs. And it costs a lot; like our sanity, peace, relationships, and, any sense of serenity. But still we hold on...and on...and on. Afraid to give up the dream even though we know it's fear-based and illusory.

So the question becomes, do we really want to have a different perception than the one we have been clinging to? Do we really want to "give up all we have known" to experience Awareness?? Do we want to WAKE UP!

It is simply a change of perception, and change of thought, a radical change in who we thought we were.. and we do this on a minute-by-minute basis until we are spending more time "there" than "here"!

It's not necessarily some big dramatic event. For most of us it's a very gradual awakening. A gradual Undoing.

10. "Although my form (body) appears to be different than others, I am no different at all."

Sorry boys and girls, the truth is, you're not special or unique. As a matter of fact, Awareness isn't even aware that "you" exist (because "you" don't). I know that you have been hearing how special you were all your life, either special – good, or special – bad, it doesn't make any difference.

You're still not special. It was a lie. A lie made up by your Ego and the Egos around you.

All this lie did was made you believe you are separate. Remember the Ego doesn't care whether it's praising you or punishing you; better/worse, good/bad, etc..as long as you're convinced you're separate from other forms.

So the body appears through our unreliable visual sense to be different from other bodies, but bodies are really all the same. They do the same stuff, they use the same senses, they have the same inner materials, and they all eventually deteriorate.

Even the body that "you" had last week isn't the same body you have now; it changes CONSTANTLY. So why are we so attached to this impermanent constantly changing mass of atoms and molecules?

We are under the illusion that "we" live there. Remember the pointing exercise? We believe this made up concept called "mind" (thoughts and emotions) is "housed" in this made up concept called "body". There is absolutely no factual evidence for this assumption.

But like good little Do-Bees, we just believe it because someone (or a lot of people) told us that.

To complicate your thought processes around this a little further, I would also like to suggest that we are no different from other animal forms, plant life, worms, and even rocks. Yes we would like to think we are bigger and better, more improved, more whatever than the other forms.

Now when you can fly on your own like our feathered friends do, or when you can swim underwater constantly like our finned friends do, THEN I could consider believing you.

Or even if you could just unfold in an array of multivariate colors and fragrances like flowers do, then I might at least give your assertion some credence, but I'm guessing I will be waiting for a long time for these to happen.

Let's look at the inanimate forms, rocks, and such. When you have been around for three or four hundred years like many rock formations have, then maybe.

How about this, can you just shine with intensity and brilliance like the sun for a few seconds? Then I would definitely believe you! (Well, probably not, but it would be fun seeing you try and convince me.)

The point being, where did we get this ridiculous idea that we're the "improved version" of all animate and inanimate forms that we are aware of? Because we can think? Well, based on all the previous material in this book, we know where that has gotten us. Nowhere! Zero! Zip!

All we can "think" about is our Ego illusion. Because we can "talk" ? Wow, isn't that something. We have gotten together and decided a number of intelligible sounds have a meaning (although we can never agree on all those meanings).

And then we do terrible things to each other because either we can't agree on the meaning (like "freedom" or "the pursuit of happiness" for example), or decide the meanings only apply to some forms, not all.

We have pretty much made a disaster over the disagreements around words and concepts. I'm not sure I would really call that "ability" we have "improved".

So we're looking at all being the same here. For many, not a pleasant thought.

Another way of looking at this concept of no fundamental difference is to consider the following:

It's the old three blind men and an elephant story. You've heard that one, right? The story goes that there were these three blind men standing around in the marketplace one day discussing, guess what... the nature of reality.

Each certainly had their opinions and they were quite astute; having been blind from birth they had developed an extraordinary sense of touch. You could hand them a kind of apple and they could tell you exactly what kind it was just by feeling it.

Once someone brought them an ancient chalice made out of pure gold and they could not only tell it was pure gold, but by feeling the ornate carvings on the chalice they could tell who made the chalice and what year it was made.

They were known far and wide for their ability to discern the nature of something by just feeling it although they had never actually seen it.

A young elephant herder (Yes, they do have elephant herders) came to town from far away. He was riding the largest elephant known to man. Much, much larger than the smaller elephants generally described.

Everyone was amazed, because not only were elephants very uncommon in this region, but no one had EVER seen an elephant this BIG! It was three or four times the size of a typical elephant. I mean, we are talking about a giant elephant!

The elephant herder had left his elephant on the outskirts of town (because it was almost too big to come into town!) and was walking through the market place. He overheard these three men praising each other for their ability to discern the nature of reality by touch.

He thought to himself, "I will test these guys ability to discern the nature of reality by touch."

He approached the three men and told them he had something they had never been exposed to and never touched, and offered them a bag of diamonds each if they could discern the nature of this object.

They quickly agreed, knowing they had the gift of touch, He led the three men to the outskirts of town and led each man, one at a time, up to the elephant.

He led the first man up to the elephant's trunk and placed the mans hands on the trunk. The man jumped back quickly and said, "Why did you lead me up to this giant swaying snake? It is a Python and may very well eat me!"

He then led the second man up to the elephant and placed the mans hands on one of the legs of the elephant.

He laughed out loud at the first man and said, "How silly you are. You have clearly lost your gift of discernment through touch. This is a very large soft barked tree. Notice how firm and solid it is."

He then led the third man to the tail of the elephant. The third man placed his hands around the elephant's tail, started laughing, and said, "What is wrong with the two of you? Have you gone mad? A swaying anaconda? A tree? This is clearly just a very thick piece of rope!"

Needless to say, all men left the scene without their bags of diamonds, and maybe a little less sure of their ability to discern the nature of things.

The point of the story of course, is that true Awareness is the elephant. You are one of the men, experiencing only one aspect of awareness and that is your definition of the whole thing.

In actuality, you ARE that aspect of Awareness, but what you experience is only that infinitesimal part of

Awareness you call your "world", your "existence", your "reality".

And just like the three men, since you only experience a small part of the whole, you think that is all of it. All of "It" is somehow defined by your little sense of "you".

All of our "individual" forms, all of our "separate" experiences, all of what we think is our specialness and uniqueness, are simply infinitesimal parts of one Whole. The parts are contained WITHIN the whole. The parts don't make up the Whole; the Whole is all the parts.

That is why, in reality, there are no good parts or bad parts, happy parts or sad parts, big parts or little parts, there is only ONE Whole. Your illusion of a separate self is just a misperception, or a lack of perception, of the Whole.

One more example of this part/Whole misperception and then I'll let it rest (briefly).

We probably have all been to one of those gigantic theatres with gigantic movie screens that seem to go on for miles, right?

Let's pretend you're sitting up close to the screen, just

a few rows back, and it's one of your favorite movies (pick your genre, it doesn't really matter).

Interesting side note, people who really liked a movie (or even a really great book like this one) will frequently say, "I was really IN to it!). Hold that thought for later.

So back to perceiving the movie. You're up close, you're IN to the movie, its happening all around you! You identify with the main character, It's like you are living it, it's happening to "YOU". All the emotions, the drama, the feelings, it's all happening right now, right here! How exciting!

Now, all of a sudden the whole screen goes blank, you're in a brief state of disequilibrium and confusion. What happened? Where is it? Where'd it go? Where is my experience (that I paid a lot for, by the way)?

Then another reality hits. The projector is on the outs. Electrical malfunction. It ain't coming back on any time soon. You have lost your experience.

Take a few minutes to recover from the trauma and then we will proceed.

tick..tick..tick..tick..tick..tick..tick. Ok, take a deep breath, all better now?

So let's look at your misperception of reality. First, what

you were seeing were different beams of light shining through colored films that took on forms that looked like something in reality. (We're talking about the way movies used to be created, God knows how they do it today, but just humor me, the point is the point.)

And those beams were so well coordinated it looked like the forms were moving in identifiable ways so that it made sense to you. Of course this was all happening at lightning fast speed.

The various sounds were coordinated with the lights to give the appearance of reality. That there were figures (forms) on the screen, doing things, and saying things, in a coordinated fashion. It was so "real" you were almost there!

Or so it SEEMED.

Now when the screen went blank, all was lost. Your entire reality came to a screeching halt, replaced, by NOTHING. Just a BIG WHITE SPACE.

Here's the analogy. Maybe the BIG WHITE SPACE is not nothing, maybe it is EVERYTHING! Maybe the big white screen is the Ground of Being on which your movie reality called life plays itself out. Maybe what you perceive as forms are just sounds, colors, lights, all moving in unison.

Maybe they're the NOTHING, although at the time it can SEEM to be very real and it can be very entertaining, until the electrical system malfunctions. Then you see the Reality behind the imaginary forms.

Notice something about the BIG WHITE SPACE we call a screen. It was this BIG WHITE SPACE before the movie screen came on, you didn't notice it because you were preoccupied with the drama of light and sound and movements appearing to happen on it, but it was the BIG WHITE SPACE during the movie as well. And guess what, its still the BIG WHITE SPACE after the light/sound/movement drama stops. The BIG WHITE SPACE wasn't affected at all by what appeared to be happening on it.

So our analogy, like the wave/ocean, the clouds/sky analogies all point to the same thing. There appears to be something larger, bigger, constant, that we hardly ever really "see" because we seem to be focused on the illusion that is playing itself out on the larger/bigger/constant.

So which is real? The Constant that does not change in the background, or the separate and constantly changing on the surface/foreground? Maybe both are aspects of the same thing?

I think back to one of those "religious" statements on some ancient manuscript, "I am the *Alpha* and the *Omega*, the *Beginning* and the *End.*" Hmmmmmm...

Leaves one to wonder, or wander, as the case may be.

Damn, I keep forgetting that for this to be a "book" it has to have chapters and a bunch of beginning and endings. I'm also thinking that it is probably supposed to have a logical progression. I don't think this does so maybe it's not a book.

Maybe I can stop worrying about labeling it as "something" and just continue to say what I have to say. You can label if for me later. Whew, that takes a lot of pressure off!

This is another check in. Feeling more Undone yet? Maybe I should stop worrying about your state of "Undonenes" as well. After all, "I do not know the purpose of anything". I really need to keep reminding myself of that!

So let's talk about some of the experiences you may have had, or are about to have that "point" to Awareness.

Chapter VII: The Chapter After the Last One.

Some Experiences in Awareness that you May be Having Now, or Later.

Turn away from what you perceive
yourself to be because you
are not what you perceive yourself to be.
Then see if anything else needs to be done.

I am not suggesting that you *should* have some of these experiences, or even that you *will*, but this is what I am aware of in my experience throughout this ongoing Undoing.

I have no idea what your Undoing is, or will be. You may not have any of these experiences. We will see, wont we.

Beginnings and endings

I am Aware that there appears to be less and less beginnings and endings in my experience. It used to be very clear to me when I was starting something and ending something. Of course it was a constant state of either beginning something or ending something, beginning something and ending something.

I used to be acutely conscious of when I was ending my early morning time at home, driving to work, and starting the work day. Within that work day, I was acutely conscious of when one task or event started and when it ended.

And of course I was conscious of when lunch time started and ended. Then I was conscious of when the "afternoon" began and how much time needed to elapse before the workday ended. I did the same thing with getting home, and when things began and ended there, only to finally end my day by going to bed, only to sleep and then begin the next day. Looking back, it was exhausting!

I realize I was NEVER OK with right now. It was a constant state of trying to figure out when this right now would end, and the next right now would begin. Everything was segmented. I lived by time beginning and time ending.

And it was fraught with anxious anticipation (not the good kind!) and loss (when something good ended that didn't feel good).

I also realize I was literally glued to my watch or any clock within eyesight. At one point, I had three clocks in my office; now that is really overkill!

Now, it doesn't mean I'm not conscious of my time commitments. I'm just not anxiously participating in their beginning and ending. One thing just seems to flow into the next more often, because it's just ONE thing.

I'm more easily able to do one thing at a time without obsessing about what is next to do while I'm still doing this. And I hardly ever look back to see if I should have done something differently. It was what it was.

So this is all about that illusion of psychological time. Now really is the only time there is. There really is no beginning and ending. We make that separation in our experience up.

Hearing Awareness

I notice that I hear more. Well, actually that's not true. I hear *Awareness* more. *Awareness* speaks to us continually. Unfortunately most of the time we are in our Ego illusion and can't hear it.

One thing I hear more of is silence. I noticed over the past few years I don't have the television set on constantly screaming separateness from the housetops. I don't ever remember consciously deciding to watch less TV. It's just not important to me anymore. It's amazing how much more silence there is without electronic noise constantly running.

Did you know silence has a sound? Try it and find out.

One of the "loudest" ways Awareness speaks to us is through Nature. Nature is always trying to get our attention! I find myself more frequently just stopping and listening when I hear a bird chirping, or when I see a flower blooming, or when I hear a stream or rain.

It used to be that all of these sounds were just background noise. Background static as I only heard my own Ego voice chattering constantly.

Again, I don't remember consciously deciding "When I hear this or that, I am going to stop and actually listen"; it just seems to happen more often.

Sometimes I shock myself when I realize I'm stopping in the middle of a busy side walk to listen to a Blue Jay.

Oddly it tends to shock other pedestrians as well. I'm sure they're wondering if I'm one of THOSE people who wander the streets hearing voices. Also oddly, I don't really seem to care what they're wondering anymore.

I also notice I can "hear" Awareness in others more often. As I refine this kind of hearing more, it seems that I can just hear Awareness speaking though people.

And it seems like I encounter more people speaking the language of Awareness as well. When I am "listening" to those people there is a feeling of Home. Like I've known them forever, and I probably have!

Walking with a foot in "both" worlds

Knowing that this reality is an illusion, that I am not really at home in this world of the Ego, although I continue to experience much of the Ego world, it is somewhat like operating in a dream.

I'm living out the Story of Ed, but I am more Aware that it is just a story. At the same time, with this Awareness being present, I am seeing more through this place of Awareness, my true home. It's kind of like having a dual citizenship!

Reader: I think I'm starting to get this. I'm hearing that I don't really have to take myself so seriously! I'm just playing out the story of "me". It seems like it's a drama most of the time.

Unfortunately one of my countries is a country at war, the other, a country at peace.

A lot of what would be considered "strange" events seems to happen when you are Aware of your dual citizenship. More frequent "coincidences", more intuitive experiences, less attachment to both my own Ego dramas and the Ego dramas of others.

This can be quite disconcerting and irritating to others who believe their Ego world if illusion is real. For them to believe their illusory world is real, they want you to believe its real too.

These individuals may see you as not caring, aloof, detached, or just plan cold hearted. It would make sense they see it that way. Remember the Ego needs to attack and defend, it must have enemies, and it has to be right.

So when you don't play the Ego game with someone else, it's usually not pretty. But you know...you just don't tend to take your own Ego dramas very seriously, so how can you take seriously take someone else's?

It is such a waste of energy to chase illusions and try to make them real, especially since you can't!

So I am saying this as a warning. Prepare to lose some "friends", but also prepare to gain more friends who know the Truth and are less inclined to find illusions attractive.

Enjoy the roller coaster ride, because you will be riding it.

I don't want to give the impression for even a moment that the process of *Undoing* is enjoyable and that as you gain Awareness, you will be in some blissful happy state all, or even most, of the time. Awareness is NOT, I repeat. is NOT an emotional state, blissful or otherwise.

Remember, emotions like our thoughts are constantly coming and going, they are impermanent. Your emotional state is NO indication of your Awareness one way or the other.

You can be feeling like the biggest piece of crap on the face of the earth and still be Aware. You can feel like a failure, a dummy, unproductive, nasty, mean, irritated, and all the rest of the "bad" words and still be Aware.

The difficult part of this is that when you are Aware and in those really unpleasant and painful emotional states, it can be even more painful because you are still Aware that this is not who you really are.

You don't "lose" Awareness because you are in a bad mood (or any kind of mood for that matter), you're just Aware you're in a bad mood.

You would think logically that if you were Aware you were in a really bad mood, it would be easy to change... WRONG!

Sometimes really bringing your Awareness to your bad mood modifies it, sometimes it doesn't. The function of Awareness is not to "change bad moods", it's to "be Aware" of whatever mood you're in.

Sometimes people encounter Awareness as if it were a self help tool, or a happy pill. It is neither. That is one thing I can guarantee. Been there...done that! *Undoing* can be *very* painful (Being there, doing that, too!).

Not to burst your "happy" bubble, but I can almost guarantee that as well.

You cannot "use" Awareness for anything, It uses you! You cannot "become" Aware, it becomes you! One thing I can say for sure, once you've experienced even the slightest hint of Awareness, its got you. You can never go back to unawareness ever again.

You can try, you can scream, you can kick, but it's useless. You're "It" and you cannot not be 'It". Your

Ego is dying, and it can feel like death, over and over again, until, there's little of it left. So let's talk a little bit about **DEATH.**

So If you wish to be Aware, hold on! You're on a roller coaster ride and you can't get off, and you don't know when, or if, it's going to come to a stop. "You" are not in control anymore, and it feels like it.

Are you *Undone* yet?

Reader: I'm getting there, wherever "there" is

Chapter IIX: The Rough Chapter

Ego Death.

The trap for the human is to define
himself as either "this" or
"that".
True awareness is turning away
from a sense of being some
"thing".
The body seen in this word is transitory.
It comes and it goes.

Not pretty sounding words, are they? And when we put them together it sounds like something bad is happening, or about to happen. On one level (the Ego's) it does feel bad, or at least confusing, unreal, like a "loss of control", like well...death.

So to the Ego I suppose it would be "bad". But everything we have discussed leading up to this chapter is really about Ego Death.

The ego which is annihilated in this process of ego death is not the ego of depth psychology and it is not the actual self. It is specifically the self-identity; the illusion that we have been discussing. One would think the process of Awakening is all about feeling good, in fact, it isn't about feelings at all!

It can really feel like death! **Ego death** is an experience that is said to reveal the illusory aspect of the ego. We read about this as sometimes undergone by mystics, shamans, monks, and others interested in exploring the depths of the mind.

The practice of ego death is a deliberately sought "mystical experience" in some cultures in some ways is said to overlap with, but is nevertheless distinct from, traditional teachings concerning enlightenment/"Nirvana" (in Buddhism) or "Moksha" (in Hinduism and Jainism), which might perhaps be better understood as transcendence of the notion that one even *has* any actual, non-illusory "ego" with which to experience "death" in the first place.

This experience has been referred to in the Christian mystical experience as the *Dark Night of the Soul.*

Modern experiencers of Awareness also discuss this as a typical part of the Awareness experience.

Eckhart Tolle, for example, stated that he underwent the experience after having suffered from long periods of suicidal depression. He says he woke up in the middle of that night and thought,

"I couldn't live with myself any longer. And in this a question arose without an answer: who is the 'I' that cannot live with the self? What is the self? I felt drawn into a void. I didn't know at the time that what really happened was the mind-made self, with its heaviness, its problems, that lives between the unsatisfying past and the fearful future, collapsed. It dissolved."

Tolle recalls going out for a walk in London the next morning, and finding that "everything was miraculous, deeply peaceful. Even the traffic!

Ego death means an irreversible end to one's identification with what Alan Watts called *skin-encapsulated ego*

This is the totality of your life experiences that make up your ego - your self-view of the world through your own eyes. When you take away all the layers built around your ego over time, you are faced with basic and often scary questions about your own existence. Many people would rather not think about these things, so they live their live encapsulated within the confines of ego.

A.H. Almass describes Ego Death as, "It feels as if everybody else is dead! To be completely "you" means being alone. When this is experienced, it will bring very deep grief and sadness."

You have to learn to say good-bye to everything you have loved -- not just your Mommy and Daddy, your boyfriend and your cat, but to your feelings, your mind, and your ideas. You are in love with all of these so letting go of them will feel like a great loss, even a death. It is not you who dies. What dies is everyone else. In the experience of ego death, you don't feel you're dying; you feel everybody else is dead. You feel you're all alone, totally alone. You have lost a boundary which was constructed from past experiences. But this boundary never really existed! It was just a belief.

When you experience reality as it is, there is no sense of boundaries or of being separate, of inside or outside."

Some typical experiences during Ego Death:

A generalized sense that something is wrong.

Panic that isn't connected to any particular thoughts.

Anxiety.

A sense that that something needs to be fixed, but you don't know what.

Feeling Lost.

Feeling "out of control

Wanting to run but there's nowhere to go.

None of the things "you" used to do that brought comfort work anymore.

More panic at the realization that the old way of being doesn't work anymore. .

A constant restless mind.

Although you KNOW something is wrong, you can't really identify the problem.

You search and search your mind for answers and it leads nowhere.

Feeling tired, slow or lethargic.

You feel like you just woke up in a different world one day with no warning.

It feels like there is no real point to anything.

A sense of death often accompanied with thoughts of death.

You don't know who "you" are anymore.

So there's good news and bad news related to Ego Death.

The good news is that it is temporary! (Although the length of temporariness can be quite long for some.) That's not really something you have any control over unfortunately.

The bad news is that it can be terrifying, exhausting, depleting, and nerve wracking doesn't even begin to describe it! It feels like death emotionally, spiritually, and physically is right around the corner. The other bad news is that it can happen more than once.

Reader: Great! That's so comforting to know.

So what do you do? Well, "you" can't do anything really. That's the point. "You" (your Ego sense) is no longer capable.

YOU ARE "UNDONE"

All you can do is find others who know what

you're experiencing and let them know what you're experiencing. And also it's helpful to remember a wonderful Alcoholics Anonymous reminder,

"This too will pass".

Chapter IX: We're On a Roll Now!

What Does All This Mean??

The world is merely entertainment of Consciousness.
It is just a ceaseless series of sensations.
It is Consciousness that creates
the mind, the illusion of
brain and body.
Don't be concerned about how you will act based
on your natural state.

That's a very good question. I have no idea. But to make some sense of it, it may help to look at some of the words I've been throwing around in the previous seven chapters (maybe).

You've been hearing about *Awareness, Consciousness,*

Advaita Vedanta, Duality versus *Nonduality*, and a lot of other words. As we saw earlier, words are not "It", they are just pointers to "It" So take the words with a grain of salt. Different people will have varying definitions for each of these words. Again, they are just words.

Let's start with *Nonduality* since it is pretty much the basis for all the other words. Nonduality is a philosophy that points to something beyond words and is impossible to define exactly.

A dictionary definition of nonduality, is something like "the implication that things appear distinct while not being separate" or "the indivisibility of reality."

Some describe it as "Oneness", "Pure Consciousness", "Awareness", Ramana Maharshi once defined it like this; "There is a single immanent reality, directly experienced by everyone, which is simultaneously the source, the substance and the real nature of everything that exists."

Nonduality also says that since there is only one reality, the world could not real, but is an illusion perceived by the mind.

Nonduality means "being" undivided, not simply talking about being undivided.

Analogies are very helpful in understanding Nonduality. For example, the space in a jar is really all space. We separate in our minds the space "inside" the jar, and the space "outside" the jar.

When the jar is broken, the individual space becomes once more part of all space. It is simply a mental illusion that these two "spaces" are separate.

So Nonduality is the state of not being separate and distinct even if appearing to be so. It is the state which allows us to say that there is no true separation between ourselves and anyone else or anything else in the world, for instance.

Nonduality can't be something that is used to obtain a goal, It isn't "something that you use sometimes but not at other times. Nonduality is what every moment "is" . It is never absent. It has no use, no value, from the usual perspectives of forming meaning and value. It simply is.

From a nondual perspective there is nothing to seek and "Enlightenment" would simply be a by-product; secondary effects. From the perspective of "ego", only when you stop seeking will you realize nothing was ever lost.

Reader: Kind of like the Wizard of Oz story.

This gradual awakening can be painful as one's focus seems to be shifting and sometimes appears to be absent.

Put in simple language, to experience" one's nature is nondualism. There is neither an "in" nor an "out", an "up" or a "down", "on" or "off". Nothing needs to disappear to realize that you are nonduality. It's simply an act of recognition.

Nonduality, as pure being absolute, exists in every moment of awareness. In the simplest and the most complex of human experience, the real YOU shines the same, without effort or attachment to whatever is going on "around" it. Nonduality isn't a "place" our minds go to, it is the very essence of who we are.

Nonduality is neither "this" nor "that".

Consciousness and Awareness are often used interchangeably. Again, everyone has their own definitions.

When you were a very small you were pure Awareness. Ever looked it a baby's eyes (that's a baby of any species)?

What do you see looking back at you? Pure Awareness.

That was a time long before you were trained in "thinking" (analyzing, judging, conceptualizing, learning to be separate, learning how to be in fear, etc...).

Everything was new. Actually there were no "things", just open Awareness of what was occurring. (That's why we "love" baby beings). At some very deep level, we remember "Home".

If you let go of everything you "think" you know, both in your perception of the " inner" and "outer" world, then you experience "one" world. There is no separation. If you let the mind open into Consciousness, it is then that you can experience "it" You are still Aware even if you don't realize you are Aware.

Your Ego illusions may appear to block your Awareness, but that does not change your True Reality. You are never really lost, because the real you never went anywhere.

Now, let's explore Advaita Vedanta, or simply "Advaita". While NonDuality is called a philosophy (although it is clear that it isn't really something you can put into a book and debate, as you could with most philosophies), Advaita Vedanta is considered both a philosophy and religious practice that appeared in the Hindu culture.

The Vedantic philosophy is as old as the Vedas, a large body of texts originating in ancient India, since the basic ideas of the Vedanta systems are derived from the Vedas, during the Vedic period (1500–600 BCE)

That's really, really old!

So Vedanta was the Vedic teaching, or knowledge. Ad-Vaita means the end of knowledge, the end of learning, or the culmination of all learning, which would be Nonduality.

Advaita means "not two".

Many people use the word Nonduality and Advaita Vedanta synonymously, but they are not exactly the same. Advaita Vedanta is a religious philosophy and practice that seemed to have first postulated the concept of Nonduality.

(That's probably not accurate. it is more likely the Advaita Vedanta philosophers were the first to write it down).

Advaita Vedanta teachers suggested practices to reveal the Nondual state (Yoga, among others, for example)

However, Nonduality does not necessarily have to have "religious" overtones at all. There are many modern Non Dual teachers (Neo-Advaitans) who do not teach from a religious point of view.

One again, from a true Non Dual perspective, it's all the same whatever you call "it". Remember, the words are just words!

So let's hear from some of them.....

Chapter X: This is Good to Know.

We Are Not Alone.

When the concept of "me" ends,
every "other than me" also
ends.
There is only One Consciousness.

Isn't that a wonderful thing! We are NEVER alone! Awareness is ALWAYS with us. And so you can see that neither you nor I are alone in our experience and discussion of Awareness, it is helpful to realize that neither you nor I made all this Awareness stuff up!

It's not original, its not new, its not "New Age" (it's actually very Old Age). Thinking, discussing and experiencing Awareness has been around forever.

Throughout history there have been some outstanding and outspoken expriencers of Awareness.

The Mystics, the Saints, the Shamans, the Gurus, the Ancients from every culture and path have experienced and then taught the concept of Awareness; in some cases risking, and giving up, their own lives.

You figure "It" must be real if so many men and women have been willing to die for "It" for centuries.

In our recent time and place in this Awakening, many traditional and more modern non-dual experiencers are still experiencing and then teaching about Awareness; Eckhart Tolle, Rupert Spira, Swami Chinmayananda, Nisargadatta Maharaj, Robert Adams, Papaji, and hundreds of others, just to name a few.

They may differ in what they perceive Awareness to be like exactly, their experiences, and their teaching style, but they are still all talking about the same thing. Oneness, Non-Dualism, Awareness.

Call it what you like, it doesn't really matter.

I would like to spend some time looking at what these extraordinary women and men said, or have to say. Not because they themselves as individuals were extraordinary, but because their message has been, and always will be extraordinary!

You will see that they, you, and I, are not separate, we are all Aware! All is One.

So let's begin:

A Course In Miracles

This is a course in miracles. It is a required course.

Only the time you take it is voluntary.

Free will does not mean that you can establish the curriculum.

It means only that you can elect what you want to take at a given time.

The course does not aim at teaching the meaning of love, for that is beyond what can be taught.

It does aim, however, at removing the blocks to the awareness of love's presence, which is your natural inheritance.

The opposite of love is fear, but what is all-encompassing can have no opposite.

This course can therefore be summed up very simply in this way:

Nothing real can be threatened.

Nothing unreal exists. Herein lies the peace of God.

Jeff Foster

Think of the word 'nonduality' as a 'finger pointing to the moon' (as they say in Zen) directing your attention to the wholeness of all life, to the Oneness which exists here and now.

It points to an intimacy, a love beyond words, a completeness right at the heart of present experience.

It points to where you already are. It points back Home.

John Prendergast

The mind learns to bow down to the heart of Silence, relinquishing the illusion of control.

Jesus Christ

The Kingdom of God is within.

Rupert Spira

If Consciousness believes itself to be a fragment, to be limited, to be bound and to appear in time and space, then the world will appear as the counterpart of that fragment.

Having denied itself its own birthright, its own eternal, all-pervading status, Consciousness confers this same status on the world of appearances.

It bestows its own Reality on the world of appearances and in exchange appropriates for itself the fleeting, fragility of that world.

James Swartz on Advaita

In duality, the subject, the person I have been conditioned to believe I am, takes his or her self to be limited and incomplete.

Because of this fact, he or she feels he needs objects…a house, a job, a relationship, children, etc…to eliminate the sense of incompleteness associated with his or her status as a subject.

He or she must develop strategies to obtain desired objects and to avoid undesirable objects. The pursuit and avoidance of objects accounts for considerable suffering.

Because both the subject and the objects are subject to change, in so far as they are in time where duality obtains, it is difficult to obtain and keep desired objects.

Time, the most salient feature of duality, puts considerable stress on the subject too.

His or her desires are constantly changing.

When an object is obtained, a change takes place in the subject that causes his or her relationship to the object to change.

The constant friction caused by the interaction between the subject and the objects inevitably leads to loss of energy and death.

Nisargadatta Maharaj

Beyond the mind there is no such thing as experience.

Experience is a dual state

You cannot talk of reality as an experience.

Once this is understood, you will no longer look for being and becoming as separate and opposite.

In reality they are one and separable, like roots and branches of the same tree.

Both can only exist in the light of consciousness, which again arises in the wake of the sense 'I am'.

This is the primary fact. If you miss it you miss all.

Swami Vivekananda

Feel nothing, know nothing, do nothing, have nothing, give up all to God, and say utterly, 'Thy will be done.'

We only dream this bondage.

Wake up and let it go.

Ken Wilbur

That all opposites—such as mass and energy, subject and object, life and death—are so much each other that they are perfectly inseparable, still strikes most of us as hard to believe.

But this is only because we accept as real the boundary line between the opposites. It is, recall, the boundaries themselves which create the seeming existence of separate opposites.

To put it plainly, to say that "ultimate reality is a unity of opposites" is actually to say that in ultimate reality there are no boundaries. Anywhere!

Akira Sadakata, *Buddhist Cosmology: Philosophy and Origins*

Non-duality is a philosophy of the absolute. In Buddhism, that which is absolute is true, whereas that which is relative is only temporary, a falsehood.

This idea arose from the concept that the world is characterized by suffering, and that we must seek in whatever way we can to remove that suffering.

The origin of suffering is believed to be the relativistic nature of the world. Because we discriminate between ourselves and others, pain and anguish arise.

This abhorrent world of the relative is not the true world. In the world from which all relativity has been eliminated, that is, the world of the absolute, there is no suffering.

That is the realm of truth.

Sheikh Kabir Helminski

We have a close equivalent in Sufism, the Arabic word *Tauheed,* which means "the oneness of all levels of being."

In the Sufi tradition, we understand that everything is rooted and unified in the Divine – a field of oneness.

Practically speaking, this means that my consciousness, my love, my will, my generosity, my capacity for forgiveness, all these attributes have their source in the Divine and ultimately all levels of existence, from this physical world through the emotional and mental worlds up to the subtle spiritual worlds and finally to the highest subtlest level of unity.

Psalm 139:8

If I ascend to heaven, you are there; if I make my bed in Sheol, you are there.

Eckhart Tolle

Time isn't precious at all, because it is an illusion. What you perceive as precious is not time but the one point that is out of time: the Now.

That is precious indeed. The more you are focused on time—past and future—the more you miss the Now, the most precious thing there is.

All the things that truly matter, beauty, love, creativity, joy and inner peace arise from beyond the mind.

The moment you become aware of the ego in you, it is strictly speaking no longer the ego, but just an old, conditioned mind-pattern.

Ego implies unawareness.

Awareness and ego cannot coexist.

Moorji

You don't awaken to Truth by analyzing the dream. Find out who the dreamer is"

You are now free, but somehow your attention caresses 'other' and your fascinations - your conceptual investments which spring from the belief 'I am the body' amounts to an eclipsing of your natural Self-awareness/beingness."

Forgiveness, openness and understanding flow naturally where there is compassion.

Something brought you here.

Something inside is delighted

to be reminded - you are nobody.

Reb Yerachmiel ben Yisrael

When I look at the world, I do not see God.

I see trees of various kinds, people of all types, houses, fields, lakes, cows, horses, chickens, and on and on.

In this I am like the children at play, seeing real figures and not simply mud.

Where in all this is God?

The question itself is misleading.

God is not "in" this; God is this.

Think carefully about what I have said. It is the key to all the secrets of life.

"It"

I am the Alpha and the Omega

Prologue: Apparently the last chapter was not really the "End".

When you realize that everything is
a creation of the mind, and
that you are beyond the mind, you
no longer see things as you
did.
You are now resting in Consciousness.
The body and the mind are fleeting.
That which is Aware of their
comings and goings stands
outside this.

So there was have "It" That's not all of "It" but that's a lot of "It". We couldn't possibly cover ALL of "It" because "It" is beyond everything!

"It" can't be put into words, or analyzed, or explained, or "understood" or conceptualized because "It" is beyond all words, analysis, explanations, or concepts.

"It" is right here, under your nose, always, in everything because everything is "It".

So after all this, if you're not *Undone* yet, you are incorrect. I say this because you're *Undone* even if you don't know it.

As I said early on, once you've started you can't go back. Try..You will see it's impossible!

And as you try to go back to a less aware state of being....that will be part of your *Undoing* as well. One step forward, two steps back as they say.

Of course in Reality, there really are no steps, and there's no backward or forward, but you can pretend for awhile if you like.

As A Course In Miracles says,
"*It (Awareness) is a required course.*

Only the time you take it is voluntary.

Free will does not mean that you can establish the curriculum.

It means only that you can elect what you want to take at a given time".

OK! That's it!

This really is the end!

We're (Un)done!

Reader: I will have to read this about ten more times, but I am getting "It"!

Ed Geraty

Do Some Further Inquiry, It'll Be Good For Ya.

Instead of searching for what you do not have, find what was never lost.

Wu Hsin

(I was going to alphabetize this listing, and then I asked my self, "why?" and couldn't come up with a good answer, so I didn't)

A Course In Miracles, ACIM.org

Love is Letting Go of Fear, Gerald Jampolsky M.D. Amazon.com

Eckhart Tolle, eckharttolle.com

Rupert Spira, rupertspira.com

Jeff Foster, lifewithoutacentre.com

The Gnostic Gospels, gnosis.org

John Prendergast, listeningfromsilence.com

Nisargadatta Maharaj, nisargadatta.org

Jesus Christ, I'm guessing you know where to find those books

The Buddha, I'm guessing you know where to find those books too. If not, sacred texts.com/bud/

Ken Wilber, kenwilber.com

Advaita Vedanta, stillnessspeaks.com

Beyond the Mind: The Short Discourses of Wu Hsin, Roy Melvyn. Amazon.com

About the Author

This form temporarily residing in Consciousness is called Ed Geraty.

During this brief residence, it does lots of things and plays numerous roles.

It has been playing the role of psychotherapist both in hospital, agency, and private practice settings for thirty years.

It also has the title of Interspiritual Minister through the *Order of Universal Interfaith*, (http://.www.OUnI. org) and Founder of the *Universalus Interspiritual Community* (http://www.UniversalusMonks.org) and the *Baltimore Insight Meditation Group* (http:// www.BaltimoreInsightMeditation.com) in Timonium, Maryland.

In those settings, this form creates opportunities for other forms to come together in groups to realize who they really are. This happens through inquiry, discussions, study groups, and various practices to move from thinking and analyzing to experience, the only true teacher.

When not doing this it does other things like blogging a Non Dual blog, *Not2* (http://not2blog.com), sleeping, and watching what happens next.

What this form does next is anybody's guess.

This is the "story" of the form. The form is actually nothing.